SECONDARY TEACHERS AT WORK

The first part of this book charts and analyses 2,688 working days of 384 secondary teachers in ninety-one Local Education Authorities in 1991. It shows how they spent their working lives, how well matched their teaching was to their academic background, and the balance between teaching and other aspects of their work. The analysis uses five major categories: Teaching, Preparation, Administration, Professional Development and Other Activities. The authors argue that there is an occupational split between 'the managers' and 'the teachers'.

This book is part of the *Teaching as Work Project* which has systematically recorded and analysed nearly 7,000 working days from over 700 teachers in ninety-one Local Education Authorities.

Both authors teach at the University of Warwick, where **R.J. Campbell** is Professor in Education and **S.R.St.J. Neill** is Lecturer in Education.

THE TEACHING AS WORK PROJECT
Edited by R.J. Campbell and S.R.St.J. Neill,
both of the University of Warwick

The last decade has seen the introduction of new educational policies affecting the working conditions of teachers, the management of schools, the curriculum and its assessment, and relationships between teachers and their employers. What changes, if any, have these new policies brought into the work of teachers?

At Warwick University, the Teaching As Work Project, directed by Professor Jim Campbell and Dr Sean Neill, has recorded and analysed nearly 7,000 working days from over 700 teachers over the period 1990 to 1992 in England, Wales, Northern Ireland and the Channel Islands. The research provides a detailed picture of how the teachers spend their time on work, both on and off the school premises, which the authors then analyse by reference to national policy, to issues of school management and to concepts of teacher professionalism.

The results of the Teaching As Work Project are published in three volumes:

PRIMARY TEACHERS AT WORK
R.J. Campbell and S.R.St.J. Neill

SECONDARY TEACHERS AT WORK
R.J. Campbell and S.R.St.J. Neill

THE MEANING OF INFANT TEACHERS' WORK
*L. Evans, A. Packwood, S.R.St.J. Neill
and R.J. Campbell*

SECONDARY TEACHERS AT WORK

R.J. Campbell and S.R.St.J. Neill

ROUTLEDGE

London and New York

First published 1994
by Routledge
11 New Fetter Lane, London EC4P 4EE

Simultaneously published in the USA and Canada
by Routledge
29 West 35th Street, New York, NY 10001

© 1994 R.J. Campbell and S.R.St.J. Neill

Typeset in Palatino by
J&L Composition Ltd, Filey, North Yorkshire
Printed and bound in Great Britain by
Biddles Ltd, Guildford and King's Lynn

British Library Cataloguing in Publication Data
A catalogue record for this book is available from the British Library.

Library of Congress Cataloging in Publication Data
Campbell, R.J.
Secondary teachers at work/R.J. Campbell and S.R.St.J. Neill.
p.   cm.
Teaching as work project.
Includes bibliographical references and index.
1. High school teachers – Great Britain.   I. Neill, S.R.St.J.
(Sean Rupert St. John), 1945–   .   II. Title.
LB1777.4.G72C36   1994
373.11'00941 – dc20
93–44327
CIP

ISBN 0–415–08864–X (hbk)
ISBN 0–415–08865–8 (pbk)

CONTENTS

CONTENTS

FIGURES AND TABLES

FIGURES

TABLES

FOREWORD

This book reports and analyses the work of secondary teachers as the educational changes associated with the Education Reform Act 1988, and particularly changes in curriculum and assessment, were at an early stage of their implemention. It attempts to chronicle the impact of the changes on their patterns of work by examining the time they spent working, and the work activities upon which they spent time, mostly in the calendar year 1991.

The book is in two parts. Part I provides the objective evidence, drawing on records of 2,688 working days from 384 secondary teachers in ninety-one Local Education Authorities. We analyse our evidence by drawing on other studies and the policy framework within which the teachers were working. We have attempted to achieve neutrality in this part of the book, both in the way the data are presented and in the way they are analysed.

In Part II we provide three essays on issues of policy, management and theory arising from the evidence in Part I. These essays are wider ranging than the evidence, but are disciplined by it. A sub-text of all these essays is the issue of teacher professionalism under imposed curriculum change.

ACKNOWLEDGEMENTS

We owe a debt of gratitude to many individuals and agencies, and would like to record them here.

The research was funded by The Association of Teachers and Lecturers (previously known as the Assistant Masters' and Mistresses' Association), which provided for a study of the work of secondary teachers, the data from which contributed most of the evidence in this book. Without the funds from ATL the research could not have been carried out, and we are extremely grateful to them.

Sheila Dainton, Assistant Secretary of ATL, has been a constant source of encouragement, ideas and critical commentary, and our colleagues at Warwick, especially members of the Policy Analysis Unit, Linda Evans, Ros Goodyear, Dr David Halpin, Dr Ann Lewis, Martin Merson, Angie Packwood and Professor John Tomlinson, have contributed helpful comments and criticisms of various chapters in draft. To all of these we owe an intellectual debt.

The data were analysed by means of a program specially written for us by Keith Halstead of the Computing Services Unit at Warwick University, where the data were prepared and processed for us with great patience and care. Ian Liddell advised us on statistical treatment. We are especially pleased to record our thanks to them.

Sheila Lucas, our research unit secretary, processed our words efficiently and with good humour. A special word of thanks to her.

Finally, of course, the 384 anonymous teachers who took the time, whilst under considerable pressure themselves, to provide us with our evidence, need our thanks. We hope the book recognises the nature of their work and goes some way to enabling the public to understand it better.

R.J. Campbell
S.R.St.J. Neill
Warwick University

Part I

THE EVIDENCE

1

TEACHERS AT WORK
Images and reality

Our ideas of what teachers do when they are at work may be conditioned to a large extent by the memories of our own experiences of teachers when we were pupils. We think of teachers as having fairly short hours of work, roughly coterminous with the pupils' day, and rather long holidays by comparison with other workers in service industries. Moreover, teachers are thought to have it easy in another sense; the nature of the job itself is considered undemanding, and only semi-professional in status (Etzioni 1969). The image of teaching as a 9 to 4 job, and the adage that 'Those who can, do; those who can't, teach', are deeply imprinted on the national, and perhaps the international, consciousness.

In England and Wales, the Teachers' Pay and Conditions Act 1987 did little to dispel this image. It specified that teachers might be required to work on not more than 195 days a year, of which 190 are days on which they can be required to teach pupils. They may be required to work at the direction of their head teacher for a maximum of 1,265 hours a year. Colloquially known as directed time, this is equivalent to about thirty-three hours per week, in an assumed thirty-nine week working year. Any other time spent on work – 'non-directed time' – was discretionary in the sense that it was not directed by an employer or superior. It was specified loosely – 'such additional hours as may be needed to enable them to discharge effectively their professional duties' (para. 36(1)(f)), with the consequence that the amount of time teachers spent on work beyond the directed 1,265 hours would depend upon the strength of either their conscience or their fear of facing classes unprepared.

Whether this image has ever been a true reflection of the work

3

of the generality of teachers is uncertain. It has been challenged by the only two sustained observational studies of teachers at work in England. One (Hilsum and Strong 1978) concerned 201 secondary teachers and the other (Hilsum and Cane 1971) concerned 129 junior teachers. Both were conducted in the same English LEA (Local Education Authority), Surrey, with a meticulous methodology that involved an unrecorded dry run day for familiarisation and detailed observation of each teacher on one or two working days, randomly allocated by the researchers and spread across a whole year. The observational data were supplemented by self-report records covering evenings, weekends and holidays.

The data were analysed by the use of two classification systems. First, the overall time spent on work was divided three ways, into teaching sessions, breaks and out-of-school. These were referred to as 'C'-time, 'S'-time and 'O'-time respectively. Second, within each of these time frames, the teachers' work was broken down into seventy-seven (secondary teachers) and fifty-five (primary teachers) different activities, which were then grouped into nine main categories: teaching, preparation, consultation, school administration, control/supervision, mechanical/clerical tasks, pastoral, private and unrecorded.

An important objective of this categorisation, given the value-laden nature of education, was its attempt to establish and maintain neutrality in description. It described what a teacher was doing at a given time, not why or how effectively he or she was doing it.

Further reference to the work of Hilsum and his colleagues is provided at relevant points throughout this book. There are two main points to notice at this stage. First, the belief that teaching was a 9 to 4 job was shown to be false for the teachers concerned. For the secondary teachers in 1974 the term-time working week was 46.75 hours, 38 per cent of which was in their 'own' time. Second, Hilsum and his colleagues made the point that, if all that is involved in the true nature of teachers' work was to be understood, focusing exclusively or principally on classrooms was inappropriate, because much of the work was conducted away from classrooms:

> On average only 50 per cent of the school day was spent by the teacher in contact with classes, and this fact ought to form the context for any study – by researchers, students,

tutors or administrators – of the teacher's professional role
. . . the average time spent on pure teaching is . . . under
30 per cent of the total working day. If those who train
teachers or undertake research isolate the teacher–pupil
learning situation from the wider role played by the
teacher, they will undoubtedly convey a false image of the
teacher's work. The sociology of the school cannot be
defined solely in terms of teacher/pupil interactions during
the teaching part of lessons.

(Hilsum and Strong 1978, p. 58)

In secondary schools there is considerable variation in the
amount of time spent teaching, depending upon the other
responsibilities held (e.g., headship of a department or a faculty,
deputy headship). It would, however, be wrong to infer that
only senior teachers have diffuse responsibilities extending
beyond the classroom. In their study, Busher and Saran (1990)
commented on the broader definition of the work of teaching
as applied to all teachers:

Teachers are no longer seen purely in terms of the classroom, responsible for pupil performance. They now have
many other specified duties . . . including essential
administration to maintain the organisation of the school,
attendance at parents', curriculum development and In-
service meetings, as well as preparation of their lessons
and marking students' work. Well understood pedagogical
responsibilities have been widened to include administrative, and in some cases, managerial duties.

(p. 1)

THE PURPOSE OF THE WARWICK RESEARCH

In the first chapter of their book on junior teachers' work,
Hilsum and Cane (1971) identified a number of reasons why
their research was needed. It would:

1 contribute to understanding teacher effectiveness;
2 correct false impressions of teaching; and
3 help break down the isolation of teachers from each other.

In addition there were groups with an interest in knowing
about teachers' work, for example, the teachers' associations,

teacher training institutions, employers, ratepayers and parents of pupils at school. We accept these justifications for our research also, but would want to add three others.

First, the findings of Hilsum and his colleagues need to be updated. In the fifteen to twenty years since their studies were conducted there has been a series of major legislative changes in education in England and Wales which are widely thought to have had a direct impact upon teachers' work. They include the Teachers' Pay and Conditions Act 1987 and the Education Reform Act 1988. The former altered teachers' conditions of employment, whilst the latter has led to changes in curriculum, assessment and the basis upon which schools are funded and managed. Other major innovations have included reforms to secondary examinations, especially at GCSE, and to post-16 education and training. Following the 1981 Education Act, more pupils with special educational needs have been placed in ordinary schools. Earmarked grants for teachers' in-service training, and the development of teams of advisory teachers to support schools, have also affected teachers' work in the last decade. Perhaps most importantly, the shift towards devolved management of schools has placed a substantially greater premium than previously on high-quality management within the schools. We need evidence about the extent and nature of the impact of all these changes upon teaching as work in secondary schools in the late twentieth century.

Second, public discussion of the education service has become highly charged politically in the fifteen or so years since the speech by Prime Minister James Callaghan in 1976. A series of papers and reports since then (e.g., Prais and Wagner 1985, White Paper 1985, Department of Education and Science 1989b, 1990a, 1991a) has promoted recurring claims that the education system in England and Wales is in a crisis, with standards in decline, and that part of the reason lies in the way in which teachers do their work. When Hilsum and his colleagues reviewed the literature on teaching as a job of work, they found that although there were many studies of classrooms, there was no large-scale study examining the total work of teachers (see Hilsum and Cane 1971, pp. 16–17 for details). We have similarly found that, although there has been an interest in teachers as workers and professionals (e.g., Lawn and Grace 1987, Ozga 1988, Connell 1985), in teachers' careers (e.g., Acker 1989, 1990), in management of secondary schools (e.g., Marland 1971, Marland and Bayne-Jardine 1986, Earley and Fletcher Campbell 1990, Torrington and Weightman 1989) and occupational stress amongst teachers (e.g., Dunham 1984, Kyriacou 1980), there has been no follow-up study of UK teachers to the research by Hilsum and his colleagues, despite its importance. It is therefore difficult to know whether the way teachers conduct their work, or have their time used and managed, is relevant to the alleged crisis. Is 'teacher-bashing' a fair attribution of fault for the problems in the education system, or a version of 'blaming the victims' of an under-funded enterprise (Ryan 1971)? We believe that public discussion of teaching should be disciplined by evidence and reasoned argument, and see our research as a contribution to such discussion.

The third reason for our research is that the way teachers spend their time as workers is important from two policy perspectives: school management at the local level, and government policies at the national level. Teachers' time is the most expensive of a school's resources, teachers' salaries typically accounting for some 70 per cent of a school's budget. How teachers' working time is used raises questions of a 'value for money' kind for school management. For example, what proportion of their working day do teachers spend on low-level tasks that do not require the skills of relatively well-paid graduates?

The research also has implications for national policies, especially on the recruitment, supply and retention of teachers. For example, if teachers spend much of their time on tasks they find unattractive or unrewarding, or if they spend what they see as too much of their 'own' time on work, to the detriment of their personal and family life, there may be problems of teacher retention in the medium or long term. Policy changes that increase the time spent on aspects of the job that good teachers find de-motivating are likely to be counterproductive.

These issues are not limited to the UK. Two international studies of teachers' work (OECD 1990, International Labour Office 1991) claim that increased public scrutiny of the nature of teaching, the demands it makes on teachers and the status of teachers' work are cross-cultural concerns about contemporary teaching as an occupation. One report saw a 'triad' of interacting forces acting upon teachers:

it would be . . . misleading to . . . maintain that the professional standing of teachers is unproblematic – their own complaints about status and working conditions alone, quite apart from other opinions and developments, are evidence that this is an area fraught with tension. That tension is played out between the triangular forces of the *professional competence and commitment* of teachers . . . on one side, the *professional demands* which good teaching today exert, on another side, and the *professional recognition* that teachers receive for their efforts in return, on the third.

(OECD 1990, p. 8)

OUR RESEARCH APPROACH

Our research used a similar concept of work to that employed by Hilsum and his colleagues (Hilsum and Cane 1971, Hilsum and Strong 1978) in that we took account of the totality of the teachers' work, not just their time in classrooms or in schools. Also, like them, we attempted to establish and maintain neutrality in our descriptions. However, because of the changes in teachers' conditions of work and the implications of the Education Reform Act 1988, outlined above, as well as for logistical reasons, there were some substantial differences in our conceptual framework and in our methodology.

CONCEPTUALISING TEACHERS' WORK

We adopted three frameworks to help us conceptualise teachers' work for purposes of carrying out the research. In the first, and most basic, we assumed that there were two principal dimensions in teachers' work: the *amount of time spent*; and the *activities* upon which time is spent.

It can be seen that *time* is central to our analysis of teachers' work (cf. Bennett 1978). If we were investigating most manual workers – or secondary school pupils – this point would be obvious to the point of truism. Their work starts and stops at fixed and inflexible times, often marked by clocking-in devices, whistles, hooters, bells or other signals. Breaks in work are precisely timed for these workers also, sometimes down to the detail of how long it should take to go to the lavatory. Teachers, however, are part of 'educated labour' (Larson 1980) as opposed to the uneducated labour of pupils, and their time is less obviously subject to overt signals indicating starting, and certainly stopping, times. The pupils' working day may be signalled by bells, but the teachers' working day is not. Nevertheless, time is central to the analysis of their work because, as Hargreaves (1991) argues, time is the fundamental measure by which work is structured and controlled – though, as we indicate later, the British may have a greater affection for measuring productivity by time put in, rather than output, than do their continental colleagues.

A second framework was used to analyse the time spent on work from the perspective of individual teachers. This has five levels as indicated on Figure 1.1, with the time on each descending level being a sub-set of the one above. It is, to use a different analogy, like a sequence of pictures of the earth's surface relayed by satellite, where each picture is of a smaller area, in sharper focus, than the preceding one.

Figure 1.1 is simple and rather self-evident, but it has two virtues. Time is usually thought of from the *institutional* point of view, from the needs of the school and its management (see

---

Level 1 *Overall time*: i.e., twenty-four hours per day, whether spent on work or not.

Level 2 *Total time spent on work*: i.e., all time spent on work, whenever it is spent, including school days, evenings, weekends.

Level 3 *Time spent on work at school*: i.e., all time spent on work during the school day, including teaching, registration, supervision, assembly, meetings, administration and non-contact time.

Level 4 *Contact time*: i.e., all time spent with pupils, including teaching, registration, supervision and assembly.

Level 5 *Curriculum time*: i.e., all time spent teaching and assessing pupils.

Figure 1.1 Framework for time analysis from the perspective of the individual teacher

Bell 1988 and Knight 1989 for examples). The framework in Figure 1.1, however, directs us to think about time from the *individual* point of view, how work fits into the individual's life overall (see Campbell 1992 for an elaboration of this point). This is important in any consideration of the impact of work on teachers' personal lives (see Volume 2 in this series, Evans *et al.* (1994)).

Second, this framework does not restrict itself to work in the school day, reflecting, by the inclusion of Level 2, time taken up with work outside it. We were able, therefore, to take two dimensions of teachers' work into account: 'visible' work, that is, work that can in principle be seen by superiors, by parents and other members of the public; and 'invisible' work, which is mainly carried on in private (or in professional seclusion on training courses, etc.), and not subject to public scrutiny. We have already seen, from the work of Hilsum and his colleagues, the problem with the public perception of teaching, which is almost entirely confined to the visible aspects of the work, even though the invisible aspects occupy a substantial part of teachers' working time.

The third framework refers to the different activities that teachers engage in when working – the nature of the work on which teachers spend time. It was obviously open to us to adopt Hilsum and his colleagues' category system unaltered. This had served their purpose well and would enable us to compare our findings directly with theirs. This was not possible for practical reasons, the main one being that we were gathering data from many more teachers for more days across many LEAs; our teachers were self-reporting and were not observed directly. Thus we needed a set of categories that teachers could use, without training or support, for recording their work activities. Trained researchers, using non-participant observation techniques with an agreed schedule and codings, who do not have to concern themselves with pupils' learning, can use much more sophisticated and complex systems than teachers are able to do unaided and untrained.

However, we were careful as far as possible to use a system that would permit comparison with the findings of Hilsum and his colleagues, since theirs was the only major study available, and it provided the opportunity to examine changes in teachers' work over time. Our system allows such comparison to be made, within certain limits, and this comparison is made where relevant in this book.

We therefore developed and trialled the coding system shown in Figure 1.2 (pp. 12–13). It had twenty-seven sub-categories of activity, which could be analysed separately and could also be collapsed for broad-brush analysis into five major categories, viz., teaching, preparation, administration, professional development and other activities. There were also ten additional codes to be attached to the sub-categories, to provide information of class size, Key Stage and other factors.

Our trials of the coding system suggested that it was comprehensive and yet manageable and captured most of the common activities of teachers' work. In the event, only one teacher out of the 711 (both primary and secondary) who used the respective versions of the coding system found it impossible to use in an appropriate way. All 384 secondary teachers who provided data for this book were able to use the system appropriately.

THREE PROBLEMS AND THEIR TREATMENT

There were three subsidiary issues that we had to face: location, voluntariness and work carried out during school vacations.

The first of these, concerning the place where teachers carried out their work, is a relatively trivial matter. Nonetheless, the problem is more complex than the way it was treated by Hilsum and his colleagues, who divided the time into work at school and work in the teachers' own time. Like them, we wanted to know when work was carried out on school premises and off them, and our recording system allowed that information to emerge. Work off school premises, however, does not simply mean at home. It could also include travelling to, and attending, an in-service session at a teachers' centre, following a course at a college or university in the evening, visiting another school during the day for liaison purposes, preparing for a class visit to a museum or field site by the teacher visiting it in advance, taking the class off the school premises for an educational visit, going on a residential weekend or attending a conference. To deal with this we made an arbitrary but common-sense decision. If teachers were off school premises but working with pupils during the timetabled school day, as when taking a class to the local swimming pool or a nearby castle for a history session, it was counted as being on the school premises. The reason for this was that we wished to include such time in the category of

1. TEACHING

Include activities where you are in direct contact with pupils/students helping them to learn. There are four codes:

TM **Teaching your main subject.**
TO **Teaching other subjects.**
TA **Assessment and/or recording for the National Curriculum carried out during teaching.**
TT **Assessment and testing in teaching time, excluding assessment for the National Curriculum.**

The codes **TM** and **TO** should be followed by either **3** (= Key Stage 3, i.e. Years 7, 8 & 9) or **4** (= Key Stage 4, i.e. Years 10 & 11) or **6** (= 6th form). In addition, write in the class size with a ring round it, e.g. **TM4 (21)** or **TM3.TA (21)**.

2. PREPARATION

Include activities in which you prepare or mark pupils' work, but are not in direct contact with them. There are three codes:

PR **Preparing and planning for pupils' learning, writing lesson plans, forecasts, schemes of work, organising the classroom and resources in it, briefing technicians/assistants, parent helpers, etc.**
PM **Marking work, writing comments on it, recording results.**
PO **Organising or collecting resources, organising visits/trips.**

Where it is possible to do so, add **3, 4** or **6**, as for the teaching codes above, to indicate the age level for which the preparation was being done. Where the preparation was general rather than focused on an age range, add **7**, e.g. **PR3, PO6, PM4, PR7**, etc.

3. PROFESSIONAL DEVELOPMENT

Include formal and informal activities intended to help in your or others' professional development, such as training days, all courses (including those leading to a further qualification), conferences and workshops. There are five codes:

IN **Organised courses, conferences, etc., but not the 5 non-pupil ('Baker') days.**
IT **Travel to organised courses, conferences, etc., but not the 5 non-pupil ('Baker') days.**
ID **Non-pupil days (i.e. 'Baker' days).**
IS **Meetings, both formal and informal, with colleagues, advisers, advisory teachers, etc.**
IR **Reading of professional magazines, journals, National Curriculum documentation, syllabuses/examination regulations, etc.**

Where it is possible to do so, add **3** (= training for National Curriculum Key Stage 3). Otherwise, add **0**, e.g. **IN3, ID3, IN0**, etc.

12

4. ADMINISTRATION

Include activities concerned with the routines of school work. There are twelve codes:

AA Administration to help in the running of the department or the school, unless identified in other A codes (include writing reports).

AE Administration in connection with external examinations/ course work and their moderation.

AC Pastoral/Discipline/Counselling/Guidance activities with individual pupils/students.

AP Discussion/consultation with parents.

AD Mounting displays.

AS Supervising pupils before the school day begins, at break/ lunch, end of school day, etc.

AL Liaison meetings/activities with teachers in other phases, other schools, etc.

AW Attending/participating in assembly/act of worship.

AB Lunch, coffee/tea breaks – free of work.

AF Lunch, coffee/tea breaks – which were not free of work.

AN Non-contact time – free of work.

//// Registration and collecting dinner money; and/or moving children from one location to another (e.g. from class to hall, playground to class, school to swimming baths), tidying up, etc. (The code for this is simply to fill diagonal lines in the time space, thus //////, since these are sometimes short time spaces).

5. OTHER ACTIVITIES

OG Attendance at meetings of governing bodies.

OS Work with sports teams, drama productions, orchestras, clubs, and all educational visits, etc., outside timetabled lessons.

OA Activities that you cannot easily allocate to one of the other codes, e.g. filling in this record, dealing with lengthy interruptions, and other things.

Figure 1.2 Codes for the Record of Teacher Time

normal teaching, and to separate it out from work done with pupils outside timetabled time on residential visits, trips with sports teams, etc. In this way we would avoid arriving at a total figure for teaching which was less than the actual time spent on teaching as commonly understood.

We also had to deal with the problem of voluntary work – the fact that some teachers attend courses or conferences in their own time. Should we count this as work or not? The reasons for voluntary attendance at courses and conferences are varied. Some teachers are invited (but specifically not directed) to do so by heads or LEA advisers as part of in-service training on the National Curriculum, for example; others go out of interest or in pursuit of a further professional qualification. Again, we decided to include these voluntary activities in the total of time spent on work, because it seemed reasonable to consider them as part of the professional development of teachers. They were the kind of activities that were work-related in the sense that, had our respondents not been teachers, they would not have been involved in them. Also, in-service training is more often 'directed' than it used to be before the Education Reform Act 1988. In case this is thought to overstate the total time on work, we have collected and reported the data in ways that enable the time spent on such activities to be disaggregated from the total, if it is considered more appropriate to do so. However, if *all* time spent on such activities were discounted there would be some underestimate of the total work, since attendance at courses is sometimes at the direction of the head teacher and, when it is, should obviously be included in any count of time spent on work.

The third issue concerned vacation time, when some teachers do schoolwork for some of the time but presumably do not work as long hours as during term-time. The issue becomes significant when attempting to arrive at an annual figure for the time teachers spend on work. Hilsum and his colleagues dealt with this by getting their samples of teachers to self-report on days in the vacations, chosen by the researchers. In our research we had no direct evidence about work during vacations. To arrive at an annual figure, therefore, there were two possible approaches: to assume that the vacation hours worked by our teachers were similar to those worked by the teachers studied by Hilsum and his colleagues, or to assume that our teachers did no work at all during vacations. Both approaches could have been used in our analyses, but we have used the second of the above assumptions. The annual figures in this book are simply based on the term-time figures and do not draw upon estimates for the vacation periods. The reason for this is that, unlike Hilsum and Strong, we had no evidence upon which to base vacation-time work. Our annual extrapolations are therefore on the conservative side and almost certainly lower than would have been the case had we researched teachers' work in vacations also.

THE NATURE OF OUR EVIDENCE

The Appendix examines methodological issues in detail, and a brief discussion of the statistical analysis is given at the end of Chapter 2, but it may be helpful to illustrate three features of our evidence at this point, viz., the evidence from the Records of Teacher Time, the nature of our samples and the evidence from the questionnaires.

Recording teachers' work

The teachers were not observed directly. They kept a record of the time spent on work for seven consecutive days, using a specially devised log or diary, called the Record of Teacher Time (ROTT). This required them to record the time they spent in three-minute segments, running from 07.00 hours to 24.00 hours. They thus recorded weekends as well as weekdays, and evenings as well as days. The Record also enabled the teachers to differentiate between time spent on work on school premises and off them. Figure 1.3 shows one day's record from one of our teachers, with a commentary by us, to illustrate the recording and coding system. It provides a picture of a day in the working life of a secondary teacher in 1991.

From the questionnaire data we know that this teacher is a mathematics graduate with ten years' teaching experience, who works in an 11–18 comprehensive school with between 601 and 700 pupils in it. She has an Incentive Allowance 'B', and in addition to teaching has formal responsibility for the pastoral aspects of a year group or year groups.

On the day recorded she starts work at 08.30 with thirty minutes' lesson planning associated with Key Stage 3 (PR3). Then she registers her class (/////) for twenty minutes, and then takes ten minutes doing something that she cannot allocate to other codes (OA), possibly moving to the sixth-form site on a split-site school. From 09.30 to 10.45 she teaches mathematics to a sixth-form group of ten pupils (TM6(10)), then has a break in which she does no work (AB) for fifteen minutes. From 11.00 to 12.00 she teaches a subject other than mathematics to a group

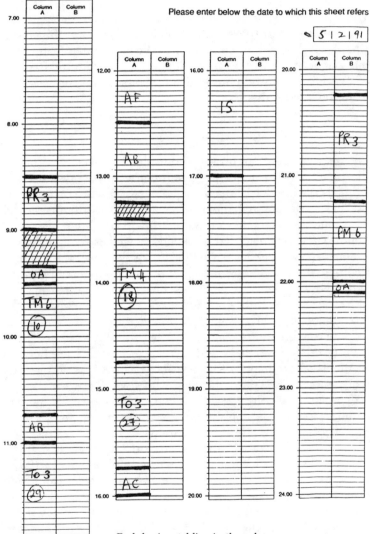

University of Warwick — Department of Education

Policy Analysis Unit
Record of Teacher Time (ROTT)

Figure 1.3 Record of Teacher Time

16

of twenty-nine pupils in Key Stage 3 (TO3(29)). From 12.00 to 12.30 she works during her lunch break (AF) and from 12.30 to 13.15 she has a break free of work (AB). At 13.15 she registers her form group (/////) and then teaches mathematics to a group of eighteen pupils in Key Stage 4 (TM4(18)) until 14.45. Then she teaches something other than mathematics to a group of twenty-seven pupils in Key Stage 3 (TO3(27)) for an hour. From 15.45 to 16.00 she deals with some aspect of pastoral care (AC) before attending a staff meeting for an hour (IS). There are no other entries before 20.15, so she does no school work until that time. The entries thereafter are in Column B, which signifies that they are off school premises, presumably at home. From 20.15 to 21.15 she does some lesson planning for Key Stage 3 class or classes (PR3) and then marks some sixth-form pupils' work (PM6), possibly from the lesson she gave at 9.30 in the morning. Then she spends five minutes on some other activity, probably completing this record sheet.

We can summarise her working day as follows:

Table 1.1 One teacher's day

Activity	Hours	% of total time
Teaching	5.1	47
Preparation	2.25	21
Professional development	1.0	9
Administration:		
Breaks free of work	1.0	9
Working breaks	0.5	5
Pastoral care	0.25	2
Registration, etc.	0.5	9
Other activities	0.25	2
Total time	10.8	100

On this day, therefore, she spent nearly eleven hours working and just under half of this time teaching. If we add the pastoral care and registration to the time spent teaching we can see that she spent 5.9 hours (54 per cent of the total) in contact with pupils. She also spent 1.9 hours (17 per cent of the total) working off school premises. The figures raise a question over whether all break time should be regarded as work, and this is an issue we explore in Chapter 3.

This day's record was simpler to understand than some

of her other days. In particular she sometimes entered two codes into one time space (e.g., PM3 and PR3) to indicate that she was doing two things at once. This would give a total time spent working which was less than the sum of its parts. The computer program analysing the time data was designed to avoid double counting in arriving at the total time, but also to take account of the simultaneous working when it occurred.

Our samples

Our sampling was unconventional in that it arose from a commission from a teachers' union, the Association of Teachers and Lecturers (formerly the Assistant Masters' and Mistresses' Association), to undertake a study of secondary teachers' workloads, following a small pilot study into the use of teachers' time at Key Stage 1 in Spring term 1990, as the National Curriculum was being introduced. This study, mainly using volunteer union members, was published by the Association (Campbell and Neill 1990) and led to seven further projects, with differing samples and data collection times. All the projects were directed by us and based in the Policy Analysis Unit in the Education Department at Warwick University. Two of the samples (Samples 1 and 2, Table 1.2 below) provided the data upon which this book is based.

It should be noted that 'national' in Table 1.2 means that the sample was provided as a result of a national invitation to members of the teachers' union sponsoring the research. Although the samples are not nationally representative in the sense that they have not been selected randomly from the whole population of teachers, they comprise teachers from 90 out of 104 LEAs in England and Wales, with small numbers of teachers from Northern Ireland and from independent schools. Sample 2

Table 1.2 Source and nature of the two samples

Samples	Source	Number of teachers	Data collection period	Number of days recorded
Sample 1	National (90 LEAs)	348	Autumn 1990/ Spring 1991	2,436
Sample 2	1 LEA	36	One week, Spring 1991	252
Total	91 LEAs	384	1990/1	2,688

comprised secondary teachers from a Channel Island Education Department. Sample 1 included some teachers in tertiary institutions, either sixth-form colleges or further education colleges.

Overall, in the studies of both primary and secondary school teachers, we have been drawing on a database of records of over 6,700 working days from 711 teachers in 91 LEAs. The material in this book uses a database of records of 2,688 working days from 384 teachers in 91 LEAs. They worked in approximately 360 schools and some 8 per cent of all secondary schools. The LEAs were mainly in England and Wales, and there was some representation from independent schools (Sample 1 only), and from maintained schools in Northern Ireland and the Channel Islands. Teachers in Scotland were not represented in our research. The research methodology is not without its weaknesses, but it is the largest empirical data-set of its kind, as far as we know. By comparison, the study by Hilsum and Strong (1978) involved 201 teachers in 72 secondary schools in one LEA (Surrey). Their data covered 201 days' observations, i.e., one day for each teacher spread randomly across the school year, plus self-reports on 194 evenings, 180 weekends and 177 holiday days.

The evidence from the questionnaire

The purpose of our research was not merely to count the hours that teachers spent on work and analyse the different activities upon which they spent them, intrinsically interesting though that might have been. As has been noted above, the 1980s had been a period of substantial and complex change in education and we wished to make connections, where we considered it possible and legitimate, between the data on teachers' time on work and the policy context in which they were working.

For this reason, the teachers completed a questionnaire. The questionnaire provided evidence about teachers' perceptions of the match of their qualifications to their teaching duties, the National Curriculum, non-directed time and other aspects of policy, in addition to information on their professional biographies (e.g., length of teaching experience, salary position) and their working conditions (e.g., class size, school type and size, non-contact time, responsibilities). Fuller details are given in Chapter 2. This information enabled us to examine a wide range of policy issues, such as the extent to which the National Curriculum and its assessment were being implemented, the match between working conditions and teachers' work, the relationship between time on work and salary, and teacher motivation, as well as some issues not directly related to national policies (for example, the match of teachers' academic background to their teaching duties, and equal opportunities in promotion). These are examined in Part II of this book. Thus we see the research as producing evidence about the actual or potential effectiveness of some of the major contemporary educational policies.

TIME ON WORK: PROBLEMS OF MEANING

A final point needs to be made in this introductory chapter. We said earlier that we have attempted to describe teachers' work using neutral categories in order to avoid importing judgemental values to the descriptive process. For example, our code TM signifies that the teacher was teaching his/her main subject, but says nothing about how well or with what purpose the teaching was being carried out. Our code AA signifies that the teacher was involved in administration to help in the running of the school or department. It signifies nothing about the efficiency of the administrative activity itself or whether it was worth while.

However, there is a particular problem with the total time spent by teachers on work. In a culture dominated by the Protestant ethic, long hours spent on work are attributed a positive value. Teachers who devote long hours of their own time to their work tend to be seen, and to see themselves, as professionally virtuous. Those who spend relatively little time on their work are often considered professionally deficient. Yet long hours might as easily be taken as a mark of inefficiency; relatively short hours an indication of business-like briskness. (Such cultural differences seem to exist in other occupations. In a study of finance managers, Neale and Mindel (1991) showed that Scandinavians interpreted long hours as a sign of inefficiency and incompetence, while British managers thought they revealed loyalty and enthusiasm.) Alternatively, for teachers, long hours might follow from loneliness or having nothing better to do than fill in time with work; short hours from a commitment to a full and active social and intellectual life unconnected with work. In teachers' conferences, where our research has been discussed, we have found head teachers loading very strong positive value on to teachers' spending large amounts of their own time on work. Some have said that they would expect teachers to work up to seventy hours a week, and would not discourage them from doing so. This issue is discussed further in Chapter 10.

It is thus easy to slip into the habit of interpreting our findings on the total time teachers spend on work in a value-laden way. We have tried to take account of the issue in two ways. First, we always refer to teachers 'working long hours', not 'working hard', to stress the neutrality of our description. Second, we included an item on the questionnaire asking the teachers to say what time they thought was reasonable for them to spend on work, so that we had some evidence about whether the teachers were working longer than they themselves thought was reasonable.

Nevertheless, it is worth concluding by focusing this point in a particularly sharp way. We have much evidence about the amount of time that teachers spent on work, and this is provided in Chapters 3 to 7. However, we have no evidence to show that long hours were associated with classroom or managerial performance, either positively or negatively. Our research did not address this issue. Whether working long hours has a classroom or a managerial pay-off remains an open question.

2

CHARACTERISTICS OF THE PARTICIPATING TEACHERS

In this chapter we present detailed information on the teachers who took part in the research. The information is derived from responses to the questionnaire that they completed at the end of the seven-day recording period. The questionnaire comprised twenty-nine items designed to give information under eight broad headings. These were: professional biographies (three items), professional context (seven items), working conditions (five items), academic background and qualifications (four items), teacher perceptions of match of teaching to qualifications (four items), teacher perceptions of obstacles to satisfactory teaching (two items), teacher perceptions of time (four items) and employing authority (one item). The content of the questionnaire items was originally created from our knowledge of the research literature and following discussions with the teachers' association which sponsored the research. It was trialled in discussion with a small group of experienced secondary teachers and minor changes were made to wording as a result of these discussions.

The information generated by the questionnaire was of two kinds: objective data on teachers' biography and working contexts, such things as age, class size, employing authority, etc.; and subjective data embodying the teachers' perceptions. The information is presented below, separately in raw form for each of the two samples, and then the summed data for both samples are presented as a percentage. Where teachers did not complete an item, they are represented by 'missing'.

PROFESSIONAL BIOGRAPHY

There were three items, concerning the teachers' sex, age and length of teaching experience in secondary schools. The data are provided in Tables 2.1, 2.2 and 2.3 below.

As can be seen from Table 2.1, slightly more than half of the participants were women and the samples contained substantial proportions of both men and women so that we were able to make gender comparisons on workloads, and on matters such as the salary position of men and women.

Table 2.1 Sex of teachers

Stated sex	Sample 1	Sample 2	%
Male	151	23	45
Female	187	13	52
Missing	10	0	3
Total	348	36	100

Table 2.2 Age of teachers

Stated age	Sample 1	Sample 2	%
21–30	19	0	5
31–40	89	19	28
41–50	152	12	43
51–60	80	5	22
Over 60	4	0	1
Missing	4	0	1
Total	348	36	100

Table 2.3 Length of secondary teaching experience

Stated experience (years)	Sample 1	Sample 2	%
1– 5	23	2	7
6–10	30	9	10
11–15	63	5	18
16–20	81	4	22
21–25	66	6	19
26–30	47	7	14
31–35	28	2	8
Over 35	7	1	2
Missing	3	0	1
Total	348	36	100

Table 2.2 shows that our teachers were also mature, with only 5 per cent of them being under 30, 66 per cent being over 40 years of age and almost 25 per cent of them being over 50 years of age.

However, age, especially in the case of women, is not a reliable indicator of experience, since many more female than male teachers take a 'career break' in order to bring up young children. As can be seen from Table 2.3, 17 per cent of teachers had fewer than eleven years' experience of secondary school teaching, even though only 5 per cent were under 30 years of age. The general picture from Table 2.3, however, is of an experienced group of teachers in the main, with 44 per cent having over twenty years of experience in secondary schools. This is a high figure, bearing in mind that the average career length for both sexes, excluding any breaks, cannot exceed about forty-two years.

There are two main implications of the evidence about professional biography for interpreting the findings of our research. First, the substantial proportion of female teachers in the sample calls for a gendered perspective for viewing the long hours spent on work, since many female teachers may have a disproportionate weight of domestic responsibilities (see Evetts 1990 for a discussion on this point). Second, findings about the long hours on preparation (in Chapter 5) would be easier to explain if there were large numbers of young or inexperienced teachers, or if there were a consistent picture, with the younger or less experienced teachers spending longer on preparation overall. This was not the case, except in respect of the very young and very inexperienced teachers – those with three or fewer years' experience – who spent more time on preparation than other teachers. Long hours on work by the sample as a whole cannot be explained by teacher inexperience.

PROFESSIONAL CONTEXTS

There were seven items relating to the professional context, concerning the salary status, the nature of any incentive allowance, whether an allowance was permanent or temporary, whether the teachers were on a fixed-term contract, the type of school, ages catered for and the size of school. The data are provided in Tables 2.4, 2.5, 2.6, 2.7, 2.9, 2.10 and 2.11 below.

Table 2.4 Salary status

Stated salary band	Sample 1	Sample 2	%
National Standard Scale	51	7	15 (15)
Incentive Allowance 'A'	45	11	15 (13)
Incentive Allowance 'B'	69	15	22 (20)
Incentive Allowance 'C'	36	3	10 (9)
Incentive Allowance 'D'	99	n.a.	26 (28)
Incentive Allowance 'E'	20	n.a.	5 (6)
Deputy head	26	n.a.	7 (8)
Missing	2	0	1 (1)
Total	348	36	100

Note: Percentages in brackets refer to Sample 1 alone.

Table 2.5 Areas for which Incentive Allowances were held

Purpose of allowance	Sample 1	Sample 2	%
Teaching a subject	23	2	8
Pastoral care	40	4	14
Administration	184	21	65
Other	35	2	12
Don't know	2	0	1
Total	284	29	100

Table 2.6 Permanent and temporary Incentive Allowances

Status of allowance	Sample 1	Sample 2	%
Permanent	263	29	76
Temporary	21	0	5
Not applicable	64	7	19
Total	348	36	100

The data on salary status refer to whether or not the teachers had an incentive allowance and, if they did, which level of allowance (including deputy headship) it was. The information does not relate to the incremental level within any status. The presentation of data is complicated by the fact that the teachers in Sample 2 were on a slightly different system of allowances to the other teachers. For this reason the percentages are presented as including Sample 2 and excluding Sample 2 (in brackets).

The comparison of the salary status data for Sample 1 with the national picture, based on allocations in the 1990 Teachers' Pay and Conditions Report (Interim Advisory Committee 1990),

Table 2.7 Numbers of fixed-term contracts held

Status of contract	Sample 1	Sample 2	%
Fixed	95	10	27
Not fixed	238	22	68
Missing	15	4	5
Total	348	36	100

Table 2.8 Distribution of salary status in a national sample of secondary school teachers

Salary status	%
National Standard Scale	40
Incentive Allowance 'A'	10
Incentive Allowance 'B'	26
Incentive Allowance 'C'	6
Incentive Allowance 'D'	15
Incentive Allowance 'E'	4
Deputy heads	n.a.
Total	100

Source: Interim Advisory Committee (1990)

shows a skew in that Incentive Allowance holders of all kinds were overrepresented in our sample (60 per cent nationally, 85 per cent in our sample). The difference in distribution of Incentive Allowances is discussed more fully in Chapter 7, p. 119.

This overrepresentation might be partly explained by the data in Tables 2.5 and 2.6. Teachers holding an incentive allowance were asked to name the main area for which it was held. Their responses, given in Table 2.5, illustrate the dominance of the non-teaching areas, with some 80 per cent at least of the allowances given for either administering a department or a faculty, or for pastoral care. The fact that administering a department is, in part, concerned with the delivery of subjects should be borne in mind here, however. The administrative or pastoral responsibilities in secondary schools tend to attract larger allowances than subject teaching, which tends to be seen as a common task for all teachers. Allowances for subject teaching are awarded where the subject requires specialist attention, e.g., Spanish in a modern languages department or history in a humanities faculty. Moreover, in Table 2.6

twenty-one teachers, 6 per cent of those answering in Sample 1, reported being on temporary Incentive Allowances, a fact which would contribute to the skew in Sample 1.

Thus, from the point of salary status alone, our sample is rather untypical but, as we show throughout the study, salary status is not an important predictor of hours on work. Likewise, Table 2.7 shows 27 per cent of the teachers on fixed-term contracts. This is a very high proportion and suggests that it should be treated with caution. It suggests that some teachers might have confused fixed-term contracts with temporary allowances. If so, it would have a similar effect on the salary status in two samples as the temporary allowances would have on Sample 1. Moreover, as will be seen below in Table 2.10, large schools were overrepresented in our Sample 1, and large schools have larger allowances available.

Nonetheless, by national comparisons this is a skewed distribution, with relatively few National Standard Scale teachers (15 per cent as against 40 per cent nationally), and considerably more 'D' allowance holders than the national distribution (28 per cent as against 14.7 per cent). Because of this skewed distribution, we have to be cautious in drawing conclusions about how typical of teachers in general are our results on the overall pattern of time on work, and especially on the distribution of work time across different categories.

We have attempted to allow for this skew in two ways. First, we have analysed the workloads of teachers broken down by salary status, on pages 120 to 132. This analysis shows differences by salary status in two ways: when salary status is clustered into National Standard Scale, 'A', 'B' and 'C' allowances on the one hand, and allowances 'D', 'E' and deputy head on the other; and by the 'extremes' of National Standard Scale and deputy head. Second, it is possible to weight the different workloads in different salary statuses according to their expected distribution nationally. This is done in Chapter 7, page 120, and makes very little difference to the overall workload.

TYPE, AGE RANGE AND SIZE OF SCHOOL

The teachers worked in a range of school types, illustrating the considerable diversity in provision in England and Wales, as can be seen from Table 2.9.

Table 2.9 School type

Status of school	Sample 1	Sample 2	%
Maintained comprehensive	255	22	72
Maintained selective	30	6	9
Maintained non-selective	8	5	3
Grant-maintained	7	0	2
Independent	19	0	5
Other	28	1	8
Missing	1	2	1
Total	348	36	100

Table 2.10 Age range catered for by the school

Age range	Sample 1	Sample 2	%
9–13	2	0	1
12–16	21	0	6
16+	25	1	7
11–16	81	18	26
12–18	19	0	5
11–18	155	10	43
13–18	33	5	10
Other	12	0	3
Missing	0	2	1
Total	348	36	100

Most worked in comprehensive schools (72 per cent), with small numbers in grant-maintained, grammar, secondary modern and independent schools. 'Other' included tertiary colleges, either sixth-form colleges, further education colleges or other institutions not seen as falling into the named categories of school type. It should be added that the category of 'grant-maintained schools' fits a little oddly into the list, since grant-maintained schools can be comprehensive, grammar or non-selective in type. However, in practice, even at the time of the research, it was acquiring a *de facto* distinctive classification, and teachers used the term as a distinctive type in completing the questionnaire.

Table 2.10 shows the age ranges catered for by the schools. This shows that 11–18 and 11–16 schools were the vast majority, accounting for 68 per cent of Sample 1 and 78 per cent of Sample 2. Small numbers of schools catered for the age ranges 9–13, 12–16, 12–18, 13–18 and 16+, again an illustration of the diversity of provision available across the country.

Table 2.11 Number of pupils on roll

School size	Sample 1	Sample 2	%
Below 300	7	2	2
301–400	9	4	3
401–500	19	11	8
501–600	29	12	11
601–700	47	4	14
701–800	29	3	8
801–900	64	0	17
901–1000	36	0	9
1001–1100	24	0	6
1101–1200	29	0	8
1201–1300	18	0	5
1301–1400	15	0	4
Above 1400	18	0	5
Missing	4	0	1
Total	348	36	100

Table 2.11 shows the distribution of school size, which was very wide. Over one in five schools had below 600 pupils and one in seven (all in Sample 1) had above 1,200 pupils. The national comparisons, based on DES statistics for 1989 (Department of Education and Science 1990b), showed that of 4,035 secondary schools, some 1,493, almost one in three, had below 600 pupils, and 313, about one in twelve, had above 1,200 pupils. Thus we had fewer small schools and more larger schools than was the case nationally. As has been mentioned earlier, this might also contribute to the skewed distribution of allowances shown in Table 2.4, since larger schools are able to provide more of the large Incentive Allowances such as 'D' and 'E' allowances.

The number of teachers working in small schools, with fewer than 600 pupils on roll, was relatively small, but is large enough to raise an issue about interpreting workloads. Teachers in small secondary schools tend to work longer hours ('beyond the bond' as Tomlinson's 1990 study put it) than other teachers, but because there were relatively few in our study this cannot be the explanation for *general* high workloads we found. Where there were differences, however, especially in the patterning of work, the numbers working in small schools were large enough to permit analysis of the differences statistically.

WORKING CONDITIONS

There were five items concerning teachers' working conditions, viz., non-contact time allocated, time spent working alongside a colleague in the same class or with a paid non-teaching assistant, the responsibilities in addition to teaching held by the teacher and, if any, what they were.

We asked the teachers to record the non-contact time that they were officially allocated per week, irrespective of the extent to which they received it in the week for which they kept records. The data are given in Table 2.12.

The interpretation of these data is difficult, mainly because it is clear that teachers who had Incentive Allowances for administrative or other responsibilities, for which they had been given relief from teaching, included such relief time in the notion of non-contact time, quite reasonably. If we had included a larger range of hours in the questionnaire item it would have generated more useful information. What we can say is that 79 per cent of the teachers had at least three hours a week of non-contact time and that two-thirds had more than three and a half hours per week. Time allocated as non-contact time may not match the time actually used as non-contact, since such time is frequently lost in 'covering' for colleagues who are absent or on other activities. Actual non-contact time is reported in Chapter 6 and was significantly below the officially allocated time.

The extent to which the teachers worked with other adults in their classroom is illustrated in Tables 2.13 and 2.14. It can be seen that two-thirds of teachers spent no time working along-

Table 2.12 Non-contact time officially allocated

Minutes per week	Sample 1	Sample 2	%
Less than 30	6	0	2
31–60	5	0	1
61–90	1	2	1
91–120	6	2	2
121–150	20	2	6
151–180	26	1	7
181–210	47	4	13
Above 210	230	24	66
Missing	7	1	2
Total	348	36	100

Table 2.13 Time spent working alongside colleagues

Joint teaching (minutes per week)	Sample 1	Sample 2	%
None	237	19	67
1–30	11	2	3
31–60	29	4	9
61–90	12	3	4
91–120	16	2	5
120+	42	6	13
Missing	1	0	0
Total	348	36	100

Table 2.14 Time spent with non-teaching support/assistant

Support time (hours per week)	Sample 1	Sample 2	%
None	301	31	87
1–5	33	4	10
6–10	8	1	2
11–15	2	0	1
16–20	0	0	0
21+	1	0	0
Missing	3	0	1
Total	348	36	100

side other teachers (for example, team teaching, or teaching with a special needs teacher or other forms of collaborative teaching) and very few (13 per cent) spent any time with para-professional non-teaching assistants, such as technicians, in the class. These figures illustrate something of the isolated nature of secondary, compared to primary, teaching. Of the primary teachers (in Campbell and Neill 1994) in our study, 49 per cent spent some time in collaborative teaching and 57 per cent spent some time with a para-professional in the class.

We asked the teachers whether they were responsible for aspects of the school life in addition to teaching and 96 per cent reported that they were, as can be seen from Table 2.15.

We asked the teachers to specify what the aspects were from a list of fourteen possibilities (including 'Other') and the responses are given in Table 2.16.

The 377 teachers who reported such responsibilities provided

Table 2.15 Teachers with responsibilities in addition to teaching

Responsibilities	Sample 1	Sample 2	%
No responsibilities	12	2	4
Responsibilities	336	34	96
Total	348	36	100

Table 2.16 Areas for which responsibility was held

Responsibilities	Sample 1	Sample 2	%
Subject within department/faculty	122 (36)	17 (50)	37
Department/faculty	151 (44)	16 (47)	44
Pastoral aspects of class/form	196 (57)	27 (79)	59
Pastoral aspects of year group	70 (20)	8 (24)	21
Pastoral organisation, e.g., house	33 (10)	2 (6)	9
Liaison	77 (22)	4 (12)	22
Community/home links	43 (13)	3 (9)	12
Co-ordination of external exams	60 (18)	8 (24)	18
Cross-curricular co-ordination	64 (19)	2 (6)	18
National Curriculum co-ordination	67 (20)	0 (0)	18
TVEI/industry links/work experience	47 (14)	5 (15)	14
In-service training	39 (11)	2 (6)	11
Deputy headship	27 (8)	0 (0)	7
Other	141 (41)	30 (88)	45
Missing	5 (1)	2 (6)	2
Total responses	1,137	124	
Mean number of responsibilities per teacher	3.3	3.7	

Note: The unbracketed figures in Samples 1 and 2 are the number of responses naming the particular areas of responsibility. The figures in brackets are the percentages of teachers in each sample having the particular area of responsibility. The percentage in the right-hand column is the combined percentage of teachers in both samples naming the particular area of responsibility.

1,261 responses (counting 'Other' as one response), an average of 3.4 responsibilities additional to the responsibility to teach. Some of these, for example, running a department or a faculty, or being responsible for pastoral organisation of a house, were extremely substantial.

There were two differences between the samples. Teachers in Sample 2 had more responsibilities than those in Sample 1 (3.7 per teacher as against 3.4), perhaps because the schools in Sample 2 were smaller. Second, no teachers in Sample 2 had responsibility for co-ordinating the delivery of the National

Curriculum, because it was not a statutory obligation in the Channel Islands at the time of data collection. In Sample 1, 20 per cent of teachers had specific responsibility for co-ordinating the delivery of the National Curriculum. Although this responsibility constituted a small proportion of responses (6 per cent), it suggests that the schools had moved quickly to identify co-ordination of the National Curriculum as a major new statutory obligation. This is particularly the case given that some 20 per cent of teachers in Sample 1 were working in institutions in which the National Curriculum was not operational in 1991, as can be seen from Table 2.10 (i.e., 16+, 13–18 and 'other' age ranges).

OBJECTIVE MATCH OF ACADEMIC BACKGROUND TO TEACHING DUTIES

Eight items on the questionnaire allowed us to obtain objective and subjective measures of the extent to which the teachers' academic backgrounds were well matched to their teaching. They were asked to define major subjects as those which they had studied for at least two years in higher education, and were asked to name only two subjects at most. In the event, the 348 teachers in Sample 1 named 481 subjects, with the core subjects of the National Curriculum taking up more than half (mathematics: 77; science: 140; English: 43). In Sample 2, the 36 teachers named 52 major subjects, with the core subjects again taking up more than half (mathematics: 9; science: 14; English: 7). The details are given in Table 2.17.

The teachers were asked how much time, to the nearest hour, they spent teaching the subject(s) they had named as their major subject(s). Table 2.18 gives the distribution across the time categories.

These figures should be treated with caution since they need to be considered alongside the figure for the amount of time that the teachers spent on teaching overall, i.e., some 16.9 hours per week on average (Sample 1) or 18.1 hours per week (Sample 2). Nonetheless, it is a matter of some interest in a time of shortage of subject skills that 18 per cent of teachers were teaching their major subjects for fewer than ten hours a week, and 40 per cent were teaching them for fewer than fifteen hours a week. There were differences between samples, with 60 per cent of Sample

33

Table 2.17 Subjects studied as major subject

Major subject	Sample 1	Sample 2	%
English	43 (12)	7 (19)	13
Mathematics	77 (22)	9 (25)	22
Computing	1 (0)	0 (0)	0
Physics	34 (10)	3 (8)	10
Chemistry	45 (13)	6 (17)	13
Biology	35 (10)	5 (14)	10
Other sciences	26 (8)	0 (0)	7
History	44 (13)	4 (11)	13
Geography	40 (12)	4 (11)	12
Social science	8 (2)	1 (3)	2
Art	13 (4)	2 (6)	4
Music	7 (2)	2 (6)	2
Physical education	14 (4)	2 (6)	4
Modern languages	32 (9)	6 (17)	10
Technology	11 (3)	0 (0)	3
RE/theology	20 (6)	0 (0)	5
Other	31 (9)	1 (3)	8
Total responses	481	52	
Mean number of subjects per teacher	1.4	1.4	

Note: The unbracketed figures in Samples 1 and 2 are the numbers of responses naming the particular subject. The figures in brackets are the percentages of teachers in each sample naming the particular subject. The percentage in the right-hand column is the combined percentage of teachers in both samples naming the subject.

Table 2.18 Time normally spent teaching major subject

Hours per week	Sample 1	Sample 2	%
5 or less	36	2	10
5–10	28	4	8
10–15	75	5	21
15–20	139	19	41
Over 20	70	6	20
Total	348	36	100

2 teaching their main subject for more than fifteen hours, compared to only 40 per cent of Sample 1.

Some 16 per cent of teachers had taken a substantial retraining course since their initial training and this may help account for some of the apparent shortfall in teaching of their major subjects, although the main explanation lies in the use of teachers' time on school administration and other activities, as we show later in Chapter 6.

The data about re-training are provided in Tables 2.19 and 2.20. 'Re-training' was defined as 'a course of substantial (i.e., at least one term full-time or equivalent) re-training or in-service training, in a different subject of the school curriculum' to that of the teacher's initial degree or certificate.

It is clear from this that a substantial minority of sixty-one teachers in Sample 1 were re-trained, 18 per cent compared to the two re-trained (6 per cent) in Sample 2, perhaps reflecting the broader opportunities for professional development available nationally compared to those in a small island authority. Table 2.20 gives the subjects of re-training of the sixty-one re-trained teachers in Sample 1.

It becomes clear that, although we specified most of the conventional curriculum subjects, almost half the re-trained

Table 2.19 Teachers who had been re-trained

Whether re-trained	Sample 1	Sample 2	%
Yes	61	2	16
No	286	34	83
Missing	1	0	0
Total	348	36	100

Table 2.20 Subjects of substantial re-training

Subject of re-training	Sample 1	%
English	2	3
Mathematics	7	11
Computing	5	8
Physics	5	8
Chemistry	0	0
Biology	0	0
Other sciences	2	3
History	1	2
Geography	1	2
Social science	1	2
Art	2	2
Music	1	2
Physical education	0	0
Modern languages	1	2
Technology	2	3
RE/theology	3	5
Other	28	46
Total	61	100

teachers were re-trained in some 'other' subject. This may mean that they were re-trained in 'subjects' like learning difficulties, careers, vocational and business studies; or they may have been re-trained in educational management, curriculum development or some other administrative/managerial area. The main specific re-training subjects were mathematics, physics and computing, in which nationally funded programmes for re-training had been provided. It should be noted, given an argument that follows (p. 38), that only two teachers were re-trained in technology.

The remaining items of the questionnaire were concerned in the main with the teachers' perceptions of academic match, obstacles to curriculum delivery at Key Stage 3 and their own time spent on work. In addition they were asked to name their employing education authority.

SUBJECTIVE MATCH OF ACADEMIC BACKGROUND TO TEACHING DUTIES

Teachers were asked how far they considered their academic background from initial training/degree was well matched to their current teaching. This was intended to elicit *subjective* perceptions of match to complement the objective data referred to above. The figures are given in Table 2.21.

It is a matter of some interest that 40 per cent of the teachers thought that their academic background was well matched to no more than half, or to only a small amount, of the teaching that they were required to carry out. Twenty-five per cent perceived their backgrounds as well matched to only a small amount of their teaching. This is a different picture from that

Table 2.21 Perceptions of degree of match of academic background to teaching duties

Match	Sample 1	Sample 2	%
Well matched	62	5	17
Well matched to most	141	18	41
Well matched to only half	53	4	15
Well matched to a small amount	87	9	25
Missing	5	0	1
Total	348	36	100

which was obtained from defining match objectively by reference to the major subject of initial training (Table 2.18) and it suggests a poorer match.

Teachers were asked which of the National Curriculum foundation subjects they spent some time each week teaching to pupils in Years 7–11. In Sample 1, 299 of the teachers replied, giving 386 responses overall. In Sample 2, 32 teachers replied, giving 44 responses. Presumably most of the non-respondents were teaching in post-16 settings or were teaching non-foundation subjects such as RE, economics, classics, etc. The figures overall are given in Table 2.22.

In addition to asking teachers which foundation subjects they were teaching in Years 7–11, we also asked them for their subjective judgement about how well they considered their initial training or subsequent re-training had prepared them for such teaching. Table 2.23 indicates, by foundation subject, the numbers of teachers judging their training to be adequate.

The total number of responses in Table 2.22 compared to those in Table 2.23 (430 as against 359) gives an indication of the degree to which these teachers, as a whole, perceived that they had been adequately prepared by their training for teaching the National Curriculum foundation subjects. Of the 430 responses indicating subjects taught, 359 represented subjects being taught by teachers feeling adequately trained. The difference, 16.5 per cent of the responses in Table 2.22, indicates

Table 2.22 National Curriculum foundation subjects reported as taught at some time in a week

	Number of responses		
Subject	Sample 1	Sample 2	%
Mathematics	79	11	21
English	44	6	12
Science	79	6	20
Technology	36	3	9
History	38	5	10
Geography	40	5	11
Modern languages	37	3	9
Music	7	0	2
Art	10	2	3
PE	16	3	4
Total responses	386	44	100

Table 2.23 Foundation subjects for which teachers considered their initial or later training had adequately prepared them

	Number of responses		
Subject	Sample 1	Sample 2	%
Mathematics	71	10	23
English	39	4	12
Science	69	6	21
Technology	20	2	6
History	37	4	11
Geography	33	4	10
Modern languages	32	2	10
Music	6	0	2
Art	6	1	2
PE	11	2	4
Total responses	324	35	100

Table 2.24 Subjects ordered by inadequacy index

Subject	Inadequacy index (%)
Technology	44
Art	42
PE	32
Geography	16
Modern languages	15
Music	14
English	14
Science	12
Mathematics	10
History	5

Note: Inadequacy index shows the percentage of teachers teaching a subject in Years 7–11, but perceiving themselves to be inadequately trained to do so.

the extent of perceived inadequacy in training, which we might call the 'inadequacy index'.

Comparison between the two tables also enables us to distinguish between subjects in respect of perceived inadequacy. It is obvious that technology, with thirty-nine teachers teaching it (but only twenty-two considering themselves adequately prepared to teach it), was seen as the subject for which most teachers had been inadequately prepared, with an inadequacy index of 44 per cent. Table 2.24 lists the subjects, using the inadequacy index, created in the same way as above.

The explanations for differing degrees of perceived adequacy will vary at the level of individuals and subjects. Technology as a school subject has changed in concept and skills, though this does not obviously apply to art. PE is presumably often taught by young, fit teachers who were not initially trained in the subject (see the discussion of match in Chapter 9).

PERCEPTIONS OF THE NATIONAL CURRICULUM AT KEY STAGE 3

The National Curriculum at Key Stage 3 was in an early stage of implementation at the time we were collecting data (Autumn 1991/Spring 1992), with statutory orders in mathematics and science in their second year of implementation for the teachers in England and Wales, and in English in their first year. Because such orders were not statutory in the Channel Islands, the data in Tables 2.25, 2.26 and 2.27 refer only to Sample 1.

Table 2.25 Teachers currently teaching at Key Stage 3

Whether teaching Key Stage 3	Sample 1	%
Yes	205	59
No	137	39
Missing	6	2
Total	348	100

Table 2.26 Most serious obstacle to Key Stage 3 National Curriculum and assessment

Obstacle	Sample 1	%
Poor pay	4	2
Poorly maintained buildings	3	1
Low level of learning resources	32	14
Lack of time	131	58
Lack of knowledge/information	30	13
Large class size	25	11
Total	225	100

Note: Missing responses omitted.

Two hundred and five of the teachers were regularly teaching at Key Stage 3. In replying to the follow-up question, teachers who had said that they were currently teaching at Key Stage 3 were asked which one of six obstacles they saw as the most serious obstacle to implementing the National Curriculum and assessment. This was a forced choice item with no 'other' or open category. Two hundred and twenty-five teachers answered, the extra twenty presumably ignoring the prior requirement that they should be currently teaching at the relevant Key Stage. The figures show nearly 60 per cent seeing lack of time as the most serious obstacle, with much smaller and roughly equal proportions nominating low level of learning resources, lack of information or large class size. This pattern compares interestingly with that of the primary teachers reported in Campbell and Neill (1994), where two obstacles accounted for 85 per cent of the nominations. These were lack of time (66 per cent) and large class size (19 per cent), with low level of learning resources at 11 per cent, the only other perceived obstacle named by more than 1 per cent of teachers. The differences, whilst not dramatic, probably reflect real differences in teacher perceptions, given that these secondary teachers typically had more non-contact time and smaller classes than their primary colleagues.

Teachers teaching National Curriculum at Key Stage 3 were also asked for what purposes they would use extra staffing equivalent to one morning a week to help in implementing the National Curriculum and assessment. This was a less forced choice item, with 'other' as an option. Two hundred and nine

Table 2.27 Perceived priorities for extra staffing

Priorities	Sample 1 (number of teachers)	%
Assessment/recording	75	37
Smaller groups	49	24
Non-contact time	43	21
Work alongside colleagues	36	18
Other	6	<1
Total	205	100

Note: Missing responses omitted. Number of teachers sums to 209, not 205, because four teachers entered two priorities, not one.

teachers replied, and the distribution of their responses is given in Table 2.27.

It can be seen that there was a broad spread across the possible answers, with help in assessment/recording attracting 37 per cent of nominations and the other three answers clustering around the 20 per cent proportion. Again, this contrasts with the primary teachers in Campbell and Neill (1994), where smaller teaching groups were nominated by 54 per cent and help with assessment and recording by 29 per cent of the teachers. Despite the disparity in provision of non-contact time, only 10 per cent of primary teachers would use extra staffing to give themselves more non-contact time.

TEACHER PERCEPTIONS OF TIME

There were four items concerned with how teachers perceived time. One was concerned with teachers' perceptions of 'non-directed' time. The question was framed, rather lengthily, as follows:

> It has been assumed that, in order to perform their professional duties during the school day (i.e. teaching, supervision, assembly, registration, staff meetings and other 'directed' time), teachers will need to spend an unspecified amount of time preparing for such duties in their own 'non-directed' time. As a general rule, and excluding holidays, how many hours a week do you think it is reasonable for you to be expected to spend in non-directed time (i.e. mainly planning, record-keeping, report-writing, organising resources, keeping up-to-date, and all INSET)?

The teachers were able to reply using categories of five-hour weekly ranges, from 'none' to 'over 30' at the extremes.

Our intention here was threefold: to identify a measure of personal sense of obligation ('conscientiousness' as we refer to it throughout the book); to see whether there was any relationship between this measure and the amount of time actually spent on work, and especially on preparation, the aspect of work most open to teachers' discretion; and to set the measure of what they thought was a reasonable time expectation against what time they actually spent. It will be seen that the measure

41

Table 2.28 Teacher perceptions of reasonable
expectations for 'non-directed' time

Stated hours worked	Sample 1	Sample 2	%
None	10	3	3
1–5	53	8	16
6–10	155	13	44
11–15	89	10	26
16–20	25	2	7
21–25	8	0	2
26–30	1	0	0
Above 30	0	0	0
Missing	7	0	2
Total	348	36	100

was a critical one in predicting the amount of time teachers
spent on work.

The teachers' responses are shown in Table 2.28. It can be
seen that the majority of teachers (70 per cent) thought it was
reasonable to be expected to work between six and fifteen hours
a week in non-directed time, although there was some spread
of times from the 3 per cent who thought that no time was
reasonable to the 2 per cent who thought that over twenty-one
hours a week was reasonable.

If the mean point in each time category is taken as the average
for the teachers in that category, the overall average of non-
directed time thought to be a reasonable expectation was 9.3
hours per week. If this is added to the approximate thirty-three
hours per week of directed time, we can deduce that these
teachers thought that a term-time week of between forty-two
and forty-three hours was reasonable.

TYPICALITY OF THE RECORDED WEEK

Three other items about teacher perceptions of time were
designed to examine how typical the teachers thought their
recorded period was of their work generally. They concerned
the typicality of work overall in the recorded period compared
to the same period in the previous year (Table 2.29), of overall
time compared to the rest of the term (Table 2.28) and of
professional development away from school compared to the
rest of the term (Table 2.31). This was intended to obtain some

measure of the extent to which the time data we obtained from the records kept by teachers were seen by them as typical. We also intended that these items should provide some indicators of validity, since we could see whether teachers who said that they perceived themselves as having spent more or less time than usual in the recorded period actually spent more or less time than other teachers. We would thus have some check on the self-recording diary system. The responses are given in Tables 2.29, 2.30 and 2.31 below.

When asked whether time on work overall had increased since the same time in the previous year, three-quarters of the

Table 2.29 Perceived typicality of time spent working in the recorded week compared to the same time last year

Stated hours worked	Sample 1	Sample 2	%
Increased	261	27	75
Remained about same	83	8	24
Decreased	4	0	1
Missing	0	1	0
Total	348	36	100

Table 2.30 Perceived typicality of time spent working in the recorded week compared to other weeks in the same term

Stated hours worked	Sample 1	Sample 2	%
Rather similar	292	29	84
Considerably fewer	2	0	1
Considerably more	54	3	15
Missing	0	4	1
Total	348	36	100

Table 2.31 Perceived typicality of time spent on professional development in the recorded week compared to other weeks in the same term

Stated hours spent	Sample 1	Sample 2	%
Rather similar	166	16	47
Considerably fewer	36	3	10
Considerably more	130	9	36
Missing	16	8	6
Total	348	36	100

teachers thought it had and nearly a quarter thought it had remained the same.

It can be seen from Table 2.30 that the majority of teachers thought that the time spent in the recorded period was either similar to, or more than, the time they spent on work overall in the rest of the term, with hardly any saying that they spent less time in the recorded week. As might be expected if the items had good validity, the picture from Table 2.31 was much more varied in respect of professional development away from school, with fewer teachers saying the recorded time was similar and more saying it was either more or less. It should be stressed again, in respect of these three items in particular, that the data refer to teacher *perceptions*, irrespective of whether their time actually had increased or decreased. We would argue that teacher perceptions of the impact of changes upon their work are at least as important (for aspects of morale and commitment, for example) as the actuality of change. The answers reflect a perception of increasing workloads, probably associated with the reforms following the Education Reform Act 1988 and the phasing-in of the National Curriculum and assessment.

There was also, as we show in detail later (see Appendix), a consistent pattern of apparently reliable reporting in the Records of Teacher Time, since those who said that they would spend less time on professional development in other weeks were actually recording more time on professional development in the week for which they kept records. Moreover, those who reported that they would work longer hours in other weeks of the term recorded significantly shorter hours in the diary week than other teachers.

EMPLOYING AUTHORITIES

A final item asked teachers to name the Local Education Authority for which they worked. We wished to examine the range of LEAs involved and, in particular, to see whether findings on the amount of time spent on work were biased by teachers' being employed in a small number of LEAs, with possibly untypical staffing policies. The data for Sample 1 are presented in Table 2.32.

It can be seen that there was a wide spread of LEAs (n=90), given the numbers of teachers involved, and teachers from all

Table 2.32 Distribution of samples across LEAs and
other school types

LEAs contributing samples of this size	Sample from individual LEA
19	1
18	0
17	0
16	0
15	0
14	1
13	2
12	0
11	1
10	0
9	3
8	2
7	2
6	0
5	9
4	11
3	17
2	17
1	24
(16)	(Independent)
(7)	(Grant-maintained)
Total	90

the DES regions were involved in the study; the highest number of teachers from any one LEA was nineteen, with seventy-eight LEAs contributing between one and five teachers. This enabled us to compare Sample 1 with Sample 2 to see if there were any differences that might be LEA-specific. The teachers in Sample 1 worked in approximately 8 per cent of the secondary schools in England and Wales.

AN OUTLINE OF OUR ANALYSIS

Fuller details of our analyses are given in the Appendix; here we give a basic description for non-technical readers.

Our aim was to have samples of a size where statistically significant differences would be relatively large enough to be of educational significance too. In a larger sample a relatively small difference becomes statistically significant, whereas in a very small sample even extreme differences, which may be educationally significant, will not reach statistical significance.

Statistical significance is conventionally reported at one of three levels of the probability that an apparent relationship is a matter of chance. The three probability levels are five chances in a hundred, shown as $p<.05$, which is referred to as 'significant', one chance in a hundred ($p<.01$) and one chance in a thousand ($p<.001$), both of which are referred to as 'highly significant'. Thus, the smaller the probability that the finding is accidental or fortuitous the stronger the statistical significance. When statistical significance is reported it still remains to show, usually by interpretation, what the educational significance, if any, of the relationship is. For example, we report a statistically significant relationship ($p<.001$) between the match of academic background to teaching duties with length of time spent on preparation. The educational significance of this finding is not self-evident (for our view, see p. 96). Part of the interpretation is based on how the distribution of the data affects a particular analysis; examples are given below.

Many of the analyses aim to relate some aspect of teachers' work recorded from their diaries (such as total time spent on work or time spent on preparation) to some aspect of their questionnaire responses (such as their salary status or whether they were on temporary or permanent contracts). For these we used *analysis of variance*, which assesses whether different groups overlap. For example, one possibility is that individual teachers, both temporary and permanent, might work a wide range of hours so that an individual's status could not be deduced from her workload, even though on average temporary teachers might work longer. In this case, the analysis of variance would show no significant difference between the groups. On the other hand, with the same averages, individual members of each group might work very similar hours, so it would be easy to distinguish (say) a temporary teacher from her longer working hours. The analysis of variance would then show a significant difference, because it is primarily reacting to the distinctness of the groups, not the absolute difference in their means or averages. (In practice, of course, greater differences in averages will often be accompanied by greater distinctness between the two groups.) However, in the data we present there are a number of cases where relatively large differences in absolute value are not significant because the values for individuals in each group are scattered, whilst smaller ones are significant because values are clustered.

Where the groups can be ordered (for example, by level of salary) an additional test for *linear trend* can be made, to see whether, for example, total time on work is related to salary. This test assesses whether group means increase or decrease in a regular way, and can only be used when there are three or more groups. For both analysis of variance and its associated linear trend test we have discarded analyses where the significant effects were due to one or more small groups whose members were therefore likely to be atypical. For example, very few teachers said their workload had diminished since the previous year, and any response from a small group such as this would be likely to reflect personal and idiosyncratic characteristics.

Two other types of analysis were used, though less frequently. First, we cross-tabulated responses from the questionnaires (for example, age and whether a permanent post is held). Here we have used the *chi-square test* to assess whether or not permanent posts were evenly distributed, or whether young (or alternatively old) teachers were significantly more likely to have a temporary post. The chi-square test is sensitive both to the relative size of any differences and the size of the sample, which interact. This point has been discussed more fully above.

Second, we carried out analyses to see which of the characteristics assessed by the questionnaire was most closely related to significant differences in the diary records. In this analysis we aimed to pit the questionnaire categories against each other simultaneously, rather than assessing them one at a time as we had in the analyses of variance. We first grouped the questionnaire categories using *correlations*, followed by a *factor analysis*. The aim of these analyses was to group categories which are closely related – thus salary status and experience tend to go together. Where categories were closely clustered in this way, we selected one of them for use in the second stage of the analysis – for example, salary status, although salary status is a secondary effect of experience. Our selection also reflected an assessment of which factors could more readily be influenced at a policy level, if they were shown to have an effect. Policy-makers have more direct control over the distribution of salary status than the experience of the teaching force, which makes salary status the variable to choose, even though experience may have a more fundamental influence on what teachers do.

The reason for this selection lies in the second stage of this procedure, the *multiple regression analysis*. Multiple regression analysis aims to select 'independent' variables in the order of their effect on a dependent variable. Thus we might find that salary status has a powerful effect on the amount of liaison a teacher does (i.e., it is a good 'predictor'). (We assume salary status is 'independent' because taking on more liaison does not automatically guarantee a rise!) If salary status is closely related to experience, however, knowing a teacher's experience tells us little more and the analysis will therefore ignore it in favour of another variable, such as the size of the school or the teacher's sex, which gives a different 'angle' on liaison and is therefore a better predictor. Closely related independent variables are therefore effectively redundant, and may be misleading. For example, considering the duo of salary status and experience, the analysis may relate one dependent variable most closely to salary, and another to experience. As explained above, the remaining variable will now be excluded although, considered independently, it would be a good predictor. It is therefore better to choose one variable to represent the composite group.

3

TOTAL TIME ON WORK

This chapter reports the findings about the total time spent on work by the secondary teachers. In addition to the time spent on work at school, it includes time spent on work away from school, in the evenings and at weekends. We might think of this as the 'extensiveness' of teachers' work, in that we have been measuring the number of hours per week that teachers spend on their work. The cautions we have expressed in Chapter 1 (p. 20) about interpreting these figures should be borne in mind here. The findings are derived from the two studies of secondary teachers' work which all used a similar methodology involving logging time on the specially devised Record of Teacher Time, outlined in Chapter 1. The data were collected over the period from the second half of the Autumn term 1990 to the end of the Spring term 1991. The data were therefore gathered over approximately fifteen term-time weeks, equivalent to 40 per cent of the teaching year. The samples had different characteristics and we provide brief details here before presenting the general findings.

SAMPLES

Sample 1

In Autumn term 1990 and Spring term 1991 we carried out a study of the use of secondary teachers' time. The teachers were working in a range of schools and tertiary institutions (see Chapter 2) but the majority, nearly 70 per cent, were working in comprehensive schools catering for either 11–16-year-olds or 11–18-year-olds. The sample comprised 348 teachers in ninety

49

LEAs in England, Northern Ireland and Wales, who kept a daily log of the time spent on work for seven consecutive days in the Autumn or Spring term, and completed a questionnaire. The sample comprised volunteers from the teachers' union which had commissioned the research, the Association of Teachers and Lecturers (previously called the Assistant Masters' and Mistresses' Association). The data collected showed the teachers working 54.4 hours per week.

Sample 2

The second sample consisted of thirty-six teachers from one mainly rural education department in the Channel Islands. It comprised 14 per cent of secondary teachers in the department. They were selected randomly by the LEA after agreement in principle had been negotiated with teacher representatives. These teachers differed from the mainland teachers in two respects: they were not implementing their version of the National Curriculum in 1991, and they were not required to collect dinner monies during registration time. The data were collected in one week of Spring term 1991 and showed the teachers working for 53.8 hours per week on average.

It can be seen from the above that we had a diffused sample of teachers scattered across England, Wales and Northern Ireland, with data collected across two terms (Sample 1), and a focused sample with data collected on one week from one particular authority (Sample 2).

DATA ANALYSIS

The data in both studies were collected by questionnaire and Record of Teacher Time. We were able to gather records of the time spent on work over seven consecutive days for each teacher, from 07.00 to 24.00. These time data were analysed in five basic ways:

1 Total time spent on work overall.
2 Time spent on five main categories, viz., teaching, preparation, administration, professional development and other activities.
3 Within each main category, time spent on further sub-categories, numbering twenty-seven in all. These are shown

in the coding system provided as Figure 1.2 on pages 12–13 in Chapter 1.

4 Time spent in 1, 2 and 3 above, on weekends and weekdays.
5 Time spent in 1, 2 and 3 above, on school premises and off school premises, the latter mainly at home. This distinction approximates to the difference between directed and non-directed time.

In addition, for two main categories, viz., teaching and preparation, and one sub-category, in-service training, we were able to obtain records showing which broad age range of pupil was involved. The three broad age ranges we used were Key Stage 3 (11–13 years), Key Stage 4 (14–16 years) and sixth form (16–19 years). Thus we could examine how much time was spent on teaching, preparing and in-service training for any particular age range. Moreover, in respect of teaching, we were also able to obtain records of the size of group taught. This provided us with the basis for examining how many pupils a teacher taught over a week.

TOTAL TIME ON WORK OVERALL

The summary data from our two samples of teachers are provided in Table 3.1. The figures for total time on work are expressed as mean hours per week. If we calculate the weighted mean for the two samples, i.e., for all 384 teachers, the weekly figure was 54.3 hours per week during term-time.

This weekly figure includes time spent on work during the

Table 3.1 Mean time spent on work overall for the two samples

Sample	Time on work overall (hours per week)
Sample 1 (n = 348)	54.4
Sample 2 (n = 36)	53.8
All (n = 384)	54.3

weekend as well as during the weekday. However, one useful way to think about the teachers' work in comparison with other workers is to calculate a 'working weekday equivalent' – to assume that the teachers were working these hours in the weekdays only, leaving their weekends free of work. On this basis the teachers were working the equivalent of 10.9 hours per weekday.

These hours seem long by comparison with those worked by secondary teachers in the study by Hilsum and Strong, where the comparable weekly figure was 46.75 hours (see Hilsum and Strong 1978, p. 65). This is more than seven and a half hours per week fewer than our teachers worked. The hours were also longer than those reported for a range of workers in a study for the Equal Opportunities Commission (Marsh 1991).

The obvious explanation for the increase since 1976 is that the work requirements have changed following the education legislation outlined in Chapter 1. In particular, the introduction of the National Curriculum, new forms of assessment at the end of compulsory schooling, devolved management responsibilities and new syllabuses in the 16–19 age range are widely acknowledged to have increased teacher workloads.

Nonetheless, we were concerned that, because of our sampling methods, or because of our different instruments, some bias had entered our figures. We examine this in detail in the Appendix but at this stage we would make three points. First, the means for the teachers in both samples are fairly similar, even though the sampling process was different in each case. Second, two self-report surveys, conducted within the same period (Lowe 1991, NAS/UWT 1991) produced weekly term-time figures of 55.1 and 52.8 hours respectively for secondary teachers. Given the different samples and methodologies, these figures are fairly similar to ours. These studies, like ours, included breaks, an issue which is discussed below (pp. 66–7). Thus, although there may be some range of estimates about precisely how much time was spent on work overall by secondary teachers in 1991, there seems little doubt that it had increased substantially since 1976.

It might be argued that the long hours reported were voluntary, in the sense that teachers had autonomy over their own time and that no one was forcing them to work beyond their directed time. There are two points to make here. First, such a position ignores the contractual element of non-directed time which, for teachers in England and Wales, is defined as: 'such additional hours as may be needed to enable (teachers) to discharge effectively (their) professional duties' (Department of Education and Science 1989a, para. 36(1)(f)). In this respect, teachers are motivated by the sense of obligation to the pupils' needs, as we show later (Chapter 10).

The second point is whether the hours worked by the teachers were seen by them as voluntary. We wanted evidence about the willingness of the teachers to work long hours, and for this purpose had included an item on the questionnaire asking the teachers how many hours a week of their own time they considered it was reasonable for them to be expected to devote to work (see p. 41 for detailed wording). We interpreted the answers as an index of professional 'conscientiousness' (see Chapter 10 for a fuller discussion of this idea). The answers to this question showed that, on average, teachers thought it reasonable to be expected to work for just over nine hours a week beyond their directed time of thirty-three hours a week. This means that the teachers thought an average of about forty-two or forty-three hours a week was reasonable (close to Hilsum and Strong's 1978 figure). As we have seen, the actual average was significantly more than this – about eleven hours a week more – and we take this to mean that, on average, most teachers were working for substantially longer hours than they considered reasonable.

INDIVIDUAL VARIATION

The means above disguise very great variation between individual teachers. Table 3.2 gives the mean minimum and maximum times, in hours per day, recorded in each of the samples.

It can be seen that the difference in total time on work between the individual teachers at the extremes was very great,

Table 3.2 Mean, minimum and maximum time spent on work overall

Sample	Hours per day		
	Mean	Minimum	Maximum
Sample 1	7.8	4.25	13.25
Sample 2	7.7	5.9	9.4

equivalent to over nine hours a day for a seven-day week in the case of Sample 1, and three-and-a-half hours a day in Sample 2. The enormous difference in Sample 1 is explicable by the fact that the individual working an average of over thirteen hours a day had spent the whole weekend on a residential course, though a somewhat wider range would be expected anyway in the larger sample.

Another, more detailed, way of showing the variation is as in Figures 3.1 and 3.2 below, where the time spent by all teachers is represented in two histograms, one for each of the samples. They show the spread of hours in each sample. The total time on work spent by teachers has been clustered into groups of five hours each for this purpose.

These show that for Sample 1 the top 20 per cent of teachers were working for 67 hours per week on average, whilst the bottom 20 per cent were working for 45 hours per week. For Sample 2 the respective figures were 64 hours and 47 hours.

This variation, which is a much more interesting finding in our view than the general average, provided us with one of the

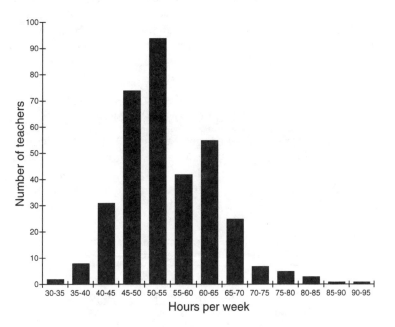

Figure 3.1 Distribution of individual workloads (Sample 1)

54

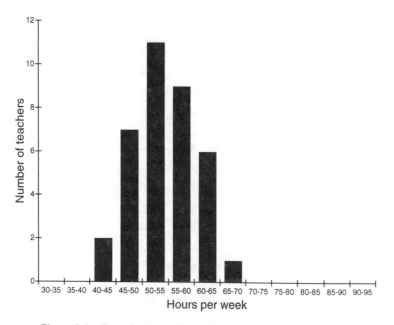

Figure 3.2 Distribution of individual workloads (Sample 2)

puzzles in our research. If we exclude deputy heads, then despite some differences in responsibilities, e.g., for administration, these teachers were all fundamentally engaged in the same job; they were all teachers in secondary schools. We do not know if those working shorter hours were less effective as teachers than others. Longer hours were not consistently related to salary status or responsibility, except in the case of deputy heads, in Sample 1, who worked longer hours than other teachers. Sample 2 did not have sufficient numbers of senior staff to enable statistical comparison of this kind. In Sample 1, longer hours were significantly ($p<.001$ linear trend) associated with what we have called 'conscientiousness' – the perception amongst teachers of the number of hours it was reasonable for them to be expected to spend on work in their own time. In Sample 2 'conscientiousness' was significantly ($p<.05$ linear trend) associated with longer hours on work off school premises. In both samples the longer teachers thought it was reasonable for them to be expected to work in their own time, the longer they actually worked. See Chapter 10 for further discussion of 'conscientiousness'. The only other variables associated with long hours were school type and size, both of which affected very small numbers of teachers. Teachers in independent schools (n=19) worked significantly longer (p<.001, analysis of variance) than teachers in other schools; teachers in small schools, especially those below 400 pupils, worked significantly longer (p<.01) than teachers in larger schools.

TIME ON MAIN CATEGORIES

So far we have provided data on the total time spent on work. However, the total is made up of time spent across five main categories of work. Table 3.3 below shows the way time was distributed between these five main categories of teachers' work, according to our coding system. These were teaching, preparation, administration, professional development, and other activities. The data are presented both for time spent in hours per week on each main category, for both samples, and the proportions of time spent on them, expressed as a percentage of the total time on work.

Detailed discussion of each main category is undertaken in later chapters. At this stage we would make the following three points briefly. First, the picture that emerges from the

Table 3.3 Mean time spent on the five main categories for the two samples

	Sample 1		Sample 2	
Category	Hours per week	%	Hours per week	%
Teaching	16.9	31	18.1	34
Preparation	12.9	24	15.4	29
Administration	18.1	33	16.8	31
Professional Development	5.3	10	2.6	5
Other activities	4.1	8	2.8	5
Total time on work	54.4		53.8	
Sum of categories	57.3		55.7	

Note: In this table, as is frequently the case in other tables in the book, the total time on work is smaller than the sum of the sub-categories. This is because teachers sometimes carried out two activities simultaneously, e.g., planning lessons (preparation) whilst engaged in supervision (administration). In arriving at a figure for the *total* time spent on work overall we wished to avoid the double counting that might follow from such overlapping activities, and the computer program used in the analysis was written accordingly.

percentages in Table 3.3 is that within similar total time there were some obvious sample differences in respect of all the categories. Second, the relatively high proportion of time on administration for Sample 1 is explicable, as will be shown below (Chapter 7), by the fact that there were a substantial number of teachers in that sample with significant managerial responsibilities. Third, Sample 2 had a more classroom-focused emphasis, with 62 per cent of teachers' total time being spent on teaching and preparation, whereas for Sample 1 the relevant proportion was 55 per cent. Sample 2 spent much less time both absolutely and as a proportion of total time on professional development and other activities.

TEACHING: CURRICULUM TIME AND CONTACT TIME

Although the implications of Table 3.3 are explored in Chapters 3–7, one point needs highlighting at this stage. It is clear that teaching, what we have called curriculum time in Figure 1.1 in Chapter 1, takes up a relatively small proportion of the teachers' total time on work. It accounts for under a third of the time teachers devote to work in a week. This reinforces the comments already made in Chapter 1 about the substantial amount of time spent by teachers on aspects of work other than directly teaching pupils.

Two further points need to be made about the small proportion of time spent teaching pupils. First, there is a difference between curriculum time (i.e., teaching time) and contact time as defined in Figure 1.1. The latter is the time when teachers were in contact with pupils and was longer than the time recorded as teaching under our coding system. The reason for this is that, in addition to teaching, the teachers spent substantial amounts of time (2.6 hours a week for Sample 1) in contact with pupils but not teaching them. This time was taken up with registration and transition, assembly and supervision. If the time spent in these ways is added to the time spent teaching, the total contact time in Sample 1 was 19.6 hours a week, so that approximately 36 per cent of teachers' time was spent in direct contact with pupils. Even using this wider definition we can see that almost 64 per cent of these teachers' time was taken up with activities away from pupils. Even if we go further and include in contact time all the time spent on pastoral care and on sports, orchestra, etc., 59 per cent of teachers' working time is away from pupils. Their time in contact with pupils on this calculation is approximately 22.3 hours per week.

Second, the contrast with the findings of Hilsum and Strong (1978) is of interest, although precise comparison is difficult because of their different codings of sub-categories of activity. Hilsum and Strong (p. 56) claimed that 255 minutes a weekday were taken up in pupil contact of all kinds, including assembly. This is 21.25 hours per week, equal to 45 per cent of their teachers' working time for the whole week. The apparent difference is explained by the low teaching time by the senior teachers in our sample rather than a reduction in official teaching time generally over the period. The two pie charts (Figures 3.3 and 3.4) illustrate the difference between Hilsum and Strong's sample and our Sample 1 in a stark way.

The explanation for the difference is not that the teachers in

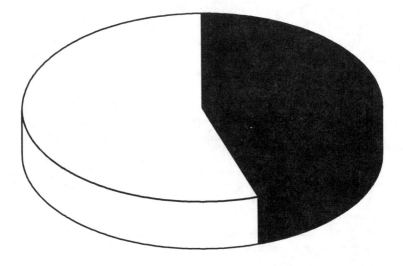

■ In contact   □ Out of contact

Figure 3.3 Contact and non-contact with pupils, 1974

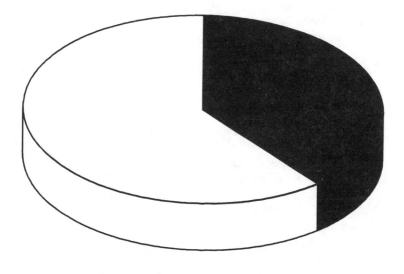

■ In contact   □ Out of contact

Figure 3.4   Contact and non-contact with pupils, 1991

Sample 1 were spending less time in absolute terms in contact with pupils than their 1974 counterparts. As we have shown above, if anything, our teachers were spending more time in absolute terms in contact with pupils than in Hilsum and Strong's sample. What has happened is that the non-teaching aspects of their work, especially preparation and professional development, have dramatically increased, and thus the *proportion* of their time spent teaching and in other pupil contact has decreased. The absolute time spent teaching by our Sample 1 teachers was 16.9 hours per week. In Hilsum and Strong's study the nearest equivalent time (viz., their two categories of teaching and organisation) amounted to 14.2 hours per week (see Table 4.2 in Hilsum and Strong 1978, p. 56). (Hilsum and Strong's designation 'organisation' mainly covered organising pupils at the start of lessons. It did not mean organising and collecting resources in preparation for a lesson, as in our code PO.) Thus the evidence is, if anything, of a small increase in absolute teaching time since 1976, together with an increase in total time on work. It is this which explains the reduced *proportion* of the teachers' time that is given over to teaching and to contact with pupils.

PREPARATION

Two points need to be made about the time spent on preparation. First, it was 12.9 (Sample 1) or 15.4 (Sample 2) hours per week. If we calculate the ratio of time spent teaching to time spent on preparation, it comes out as 1:0.76 and 1:0.85. Even these figures exclude time spent on reading professional journals and National Curriculum documents – fifty-six minutes per week – which might reasonably be included in teachers' preparation time. If this is done, the ratio becomes 1:0.82 for Sample 1 (see Chapter 5 for a fuller discussion of this point). The teaching:preparation ratios imply that for every hour that they taught their pupils the teachers were spending almost fifty minutes in preparation.

Second, on the face of it, this ratio requires some explanation since it is improbable that teaching requires such a large amount of preparation in the normal run of things. (If it did, the teachers' working week would be almost thirty-one hours long before anything else was undertaken.) The explanation does not lie in teacher inexperience. There were very few inexperienced teachers in our samples. Eighty-seven per cent had more than ten years' experience of secondary school teaching. It is likely that the hours on preparation are in some significant measure affected by recent curricular changes, including the requirements associated with the National Curriculum, new forms of examining at 16 and new courses in the 16–19 age range. These either had recently been, or were being, introduced at the time the data were collected.

If the above interpretation is correct, it might follow that the amount of preparation carried out by teachers as they become more familiar with the new requirements would be reduced. The long hours on preparation on this interpretation would be merely a 'blip' arising from the novelty of the innovations. They would not be a permanent or even long-standing feature of teachers' work. This is an assumption that has been quantified for primary teachers in Coopers and Lybrand Deloitte (1991). There are two reasons why this assumption is unlikely to be realised. First, 1991 was only the beginning. The National Curriculum and assessment were being phased in over a fairly long time. In 1991, the teachers in our Sample 1 had implemented statutory orders in mathematics and science, and were starting to implement the English orders for the first and second years of Key Stage 3. The following years would serially involve statutory orders in the other foundation subjects, and these would involve changes to the newly implemented GCSE courses and examinations.

Second, the National Curriculum has been, and will continue to be, subject to fairly regular change. The orders in mathematics and science were already altered significantly for implementation in 1993, English and technology orders were revised in 1993 and the assessment arrangements were altered between 1991 and 1992 (see Black 1992). They are unlikely to be the only changes since the National Curriculum Council has a statutory responsibility to keep the curriculum under review and, in 1993, commenced a review of the existing orders. Its interim report (National Curriculum Council/SEAC 1993) proposed substantial changes to curriculum content, assessment arrangements and curriculum organisation, 14–19.

Thus for these two reasons we think the apparently high figures for preparation time are likely to persist until the National Curriculum and assessment arrangements have stabilised and become routine. Such routinisation is unlikely to be felt as a reality until the late 1990s at the earliest, although it might stabilise earlier at Key Stage 3 than at Key Stage 4 because of the incompatibility of GCSE examinations and courses with aspects of the National Curriculum. This point ignores any changes to post-16 examinations, where pressure for change in 'A' Level syllabuses and in vocational and pre-vocational training remains high.

ADMINISTRATION

The teachers in Sample 1 were spending 18.1 hours per week on administration. Our use of this term covers, as can be seen from the coding system in Chapter 1 (Figure 1.2, pp. 12–13), a range of activities which contribute to the smooth functioning of the school but do not directly involve teaching pupils. It includes registration and transition (i.e., moving children around the school), participating in assembly, meeting parents and putting up displays. It also includes break times and non-contact time. It also includes the kind of managerial, pastoral and clerical activity normally undertaken by senior teachers, and often referred to as school administration.

The time recorded as administration included morning and, where they occurred, afternoon breaks and the lunchtime break. We were able to distinguish between time in these breaks when teachers were engaged in work, for example, planning lessons or marking, and time when they were free of work. The time in all these breaks when teachers were free of work amounted on average to 4.8 hours per week.

In Sample 2 the smaller absolute time on administration is partly explained by the fact that the teachers in this Authority did not spend time on collecting dinner money, and there were no deputy heads in the sample.

PROFESSIONAL DEVELOPMENT

The teachers in Sample 1 spent 5.3 hours per week on professional development. In our coding system professional development included in-service courses, travel to courses, formal and informal meetings, the non-pupil days and reading professional journals and curriculum documents. In Sample 2 the time spent on in-service training and travel was much lower than in Sample 1, and Sample 2 had no non-pupil days. Two of the elements in professional development, viz., meetings and reading journals, etc., might be considered as only remotely concerned with the professional development of teachers. The latter, as has been argued above (p. 60) might be regarded as preparation, whilst the former might be thought of more appropriately as administration.

The problem arises because staff meetings differ in nature and teachers read journals for different purposes. Some staff meetings concern themselves primarily with school routines, others with curriculum development. Many mix both kinds of activity. Teachers may read journals for job vacancies, ideas for lessons or to improve their professional knowledge. The case for including staff meetings under professional development is discussed in Chapter 5.

This is not a difficult problem for us to resolve since the data

62

are presented separately in later chapters in this book. If readers think that our decision to include these activities under professional development is inappropriate, the hours can easily be allocated to other main categories, as we do below, and the distribution of figures in Table 3.3 adjusted accordingly. The balance across main categories will alter, but hours spent on work overall are not affected.

For example, we can transfer time spent in meetings (2.6 hours per week) and reading (fifty-six minutes per week) to administration and preparation respectively, from professional development, for Sample 1. They came to 3.5 hours a week combined. The changes they make to the distribution of time across the main categories are shown in Table 3.4.

Table 3.4 Mean time spent on the five main categories for Sample 1, when professional reading is allocated to preparation, and meetings to administration

Category	Sample 1 (hours per week)	% of total time
Teaching	16.9	31
Preparation	13.8	25
Administration	20.7	38
Professional development	1.8	3
Other activities	4.1	8
Total time on work	54.4	105

The implications for the ratio of teaching to preparation have been discussed above. However, the significant shift of time on meetings into administration and away from professional development is more than a matter of linguistics or pedantry. It has been argued that the educational reforms in England and Wales have led to an increasing bureaucratisation of the teachers' work. If we make this assumption about meetings, represented in Table 3.4, the professional development of teachers occupies a very minor part (1.8 hours per week) of their working week, and 38 per cent of their time is taken up with administration as we have defined it.

OTHER ACTIVITIES

Other activities occupied 4.1 and 2.8 hours per week for Samples 1 and 2 respectively, and mainly involved sports, orchestras, etc., outside timetabled lessons, or miscellaneous activities that the teachers could not allocate to our other codes. A small amount of this time in Sample 1 was taken up with governors' meetings.

DIRECTED AND NON-DIRECTED TIME

We were interested in the division between directed and non-directed time because of the contractual frame within which the teachers' work had been set by the Teachers' Pay and Conditions Act 1987. We had reason to believe that asking the teachers to code which of their activities were subject to directed time would not be helpful, since many heads do not direct time at the level of daily routines. They simply direct time for teaching and for important scheduled meetings such as parents' evenings, staff meetings, etc.

In order to take account of this we designed the Record of Teacher Time in a way that enabled us to break down the total time spent on work according to whether it was spent at school or away from school. The purpose here was twofold. First, we wished to know how much time teachers spent on work that was 'invisible' to the public, and even to their heads and their employers. Second, there was the issue of how many hours teachers were working in non-directed time. We took, as an assumption, that time away from school was, for all practical purposes, non-directed time. In this way we were able to arrive at a *minimum* figure for non-directed time from our data. This is given in Table 3.5.

In addition, however, some time at school is not directed and in order to take account of this we calculated another figure. This figure was the total time on work minus the thirty-three hours that is statutorily supposed to be worked each week at the head teacher's direction. Table 3.6 provides the relevant

Table 3.5 Time spent on work: on and off school premises

	Hours per week	
Distribution of time	Sample 1	Sample 2
Mean time spent on work on school premises	39.8	39.4
Mean time spent on work off school premises	14.6	14.4
Total mean time spent on work	54.4	53.8

Table 3.6 Time spent on work: directed and
non-directed

Time spent on work	Sample 1 (hours per week)
(1) Total time	54.4
(2) Total directed time	33.2
(3) Difference between (1) and (2): 'non-directed time'	21.2

figures for Sample 1. (Sample 2 did not have contractually defined non-directed time.)

Tables 3.5 and 3.6 reveal that the teachers were working considerably longer hours than the statutorily directed time of thirty-three hours, whichever of the figures is applied. The figures in Table 3.5 show the teachers working over 14.5 hours a week away from school, mostly at home. Using these hours off school premises as the minimum non-directed time, we can calculate the ratio of directed hours to non-directed hours as 2.7:1. That is to say, for every hour working at the direction of the head, the teachers spent another twenty-two minutes in their own time.

Sample 2 teachers had slightly different contractual arrangements from those in Sample 1, and for that reason it is not technically appropriate to analyse their time in a similar way. However, despite this, there was a striking similarity between the two samples, since Sample 2 teachers spent 39.4 hours a week working on school premises and 14.4 hours a week off school premises.

However, for Sample 1, the assumption that no time on school premises is non-directed is false. The requirements of the Teachers' Pay and Conditions Act include the requirement that teachers spend 1,265 hours a year, or thirty-three hours a week in term-time, working at the direction of the head. The remainder of their work is non-directed, as defined earlier (pp. 52–3). Table 3.6 analyses the time data on this assumption. Here the ratio of directed to non-directed hours is approximately 1.6:1. For every hour of directed time, the teachers spent another thirty-eight minutes in their own time. Table 3.6 represents the more accurate of the divisions between directed and non-directed time, in our view.

TIME ON WORK AT WEEKENDS

Our final analysis is concerned with the distribution of time during the five weekdays and the weekends. The computer program was written so as to enable us to present the time data for 'real' weekdays, i.e., for the time actually spent on work during the five weekdays. It is therefore different from the calculation of the 'working weekday equivalent' referred to above (p. 52), which was created by taking the total time spent on work over the seven days and dividing it by five instead of seven. The data on real weekdays represent time actually recorded in the five weekdays. Time spent on work at weekends is similarly real. Table 3.7 gives the data for both samples.

Table 3.7 Time spent on work: weekdays and weekends

	Hours per week	
Distribution of time	*Sample 1*	*Sample 2*
Weekdays	48.4	47.8
Weekends	6.0	6.0
Total time	54.4	53.8

Table 3.7, like most of the other tables showing the data separately for each sample, reveals substantial consistency between the two. On average teachers worked for six hours (i.e., three hours per day) at the weekends. On weekdays they worked for 9.7 hours on average.

The policy issues associated with these findings are discussed in Chapter 8. At this stage we would simply note that our research, like Hilsum and Strong's, explodes the myth of teaching as a 9 to 4 job. Our figures suggest that it is more like a 9 to 7 job.

THE TREATMENT OF BREAKS

The figures for total time on work given in this chapter include time in breaks. These include time spent in morning coffee breaks, lunchtimes and, where applicable, afternoon breaks. It is questionable, to say the least, whether all time spent in breaks should count as work.

One solution would be to deduct all time spent in breaks from the total time. The difficulties with this are, first, that it would treat the fifteen-minute morning coffee break in the same way as the much longer lunch break and, second, that teachers often work during their breaks, on preparation and marking, for example. Our coding system enabled the teachers to record when they worked during breaks and when they had breaks free of work.

The average time spent in breaks free of work for the two samples was twenty-nine (Sample 1) and thirty-nine (Sample 2) minutes per weekday. This gives weekly means in hours of 2.4 (Sample 1) and 3.25 (Sample 2). If no allowance is given for the time in morning coffee breaks to be recognised as working time, irrespective of how it is used, these hourly means should be deducted from the hours allocated to administration in Table 3.3 on page 56 above, and the total time on work adjusted accordingly. This would give total time on work as 52.0 and 50.5 for Samples 1 and 2 respectively.

A middle way would be to allow the morning break of fifteen minutes to count as working time. The reasoning here is that teachers cannot leave the school during this time, and that the DES *Circular on the Length and Control of School Sessions* (Department of Education and Science 1989c) includes the morning break in directed time. The hourly means free of work would therefore be reduced by 1.25 hours a week, and the total time on work for Samples 1 and 2 would be 53.25 and 51.75 hours per week respectively.

AN ANNUAL EXTRAPOLATION

To arrive at an annual average figure for teachers' work, we have assumed, almost certainly wrongly, that no work is ever done in the periods outside the thirty-nine weeks of the teachers' working year. We have then taken the thirty-eight weeks of the teaching year and multiplied it by the average weekly term-time hours for the two samples (54.3 hours). This gives 2,063.4 hours. To this should be added the thirty hours allocated annually to non-pupil days. Under this method the annual figure would be 2,093.4 hours. Assuming a forty-six week working year (i.e., six weeks of holidays, including public holidays), the teachers were working the equivalent of a 45.5-hour week. If breaks are treated on the last assumption mentioned above, the equivalent working week would be 44.3 hours, although this would be an under-estimate because work in vacations, including half-terms, has not been allowed for in any way.

COMPARISON WITH OTHER OCCUPATIONS

It is extremely difficult to make direct comparisons between teachers' hours and those worked by other occupations because of the unusual contractual obligation of non-directed time laid upon teachers in England and Wales. However, some tentative comparisons can be made based on the information provided by Incomes Data Services (Study 517, November 1992). Three comparisons are worth making.

First, in a general comment, IDS notes that: 'The 35-hour week remains the most common for non-manual workers . . . and in many sectors it represents the norm for the industry' (Incomes Data Services 1990, p. 5). Second, the IDS study lists annual hours of work in thirteen European countries (p. 8). This shows that the range of collectively agreed weekly hours in 1992 was between thirty-five and forty in twelve countries, with only Portugal having a top range above forty, at forty-two hours per week. Annual working time in manufacturing industry in 1991 shows the majority of countries having between 1,700 and 1,800 hours, and no country with hours exceeding 2,000. The highest (Portugal again) was 1,935 hours annually. Third, the study provides a detailed forty-six-page breakdown of the basic hours worked in a range of private firms and public sector organisa-tions. The figures are sometimes weekly and sometimes annual hours on work. It is almost impossible (junior doctors in the National Health Service are one exception) to find any non-manual occupation, public or private, where the basic hours approach the level we report for teachers. This is, in part, because the IDS figures are agreed basic hours and do not necessarily reflect actual hours worked. For this reason direct comparison is not appropriate. Despite the difficulties, how-ever, the three comparisons above suggest that, despite the apparently low number of hours of directed time agreed for teachers, they actually work significantly longer hours than most other non-manual and manual workers in Great Britain or in Europe.

SUMMARY

The teachers were working for just over fifty-four hours per week, an increase of approximately seven hours on the Hilsum and Strong (1978) sample, with their data being collected in 1976. There was considerable individual variation, ranging from over ninety to under thirty-five hours. Teaching and preparation (including marking) took up 31 per cent and 24 per cent respectively of the working week, but the teachers were in contact with pupils for under 40 per cent of their working time. A large proportion of time, over 30 per cent of the week, was taken up with administration, in our very broad definition of it. Professional development took up 10 per cent of the working week, if meetings and reading journals are included in the definition. A range of other activities took up 8 per cent of the week. Our calculation is that teachers worked a ratio of directed to non-directed time of 1 hour directed to 38 minutes non-directed. Of their working week of fifty-four hours, just over fourteen hours were spent off school premises, mainly at home, and six hours were spent on work at weekends.

4

TEACHING AND THE CURRICULUM

Teaching pupils is regarded by the public as the most important part of the teachers' job. It is what they are paid to do. But two introductory points need to be made about the nature of our evidence concerning the time that teachers spent teaching.

First, pupil learning is normally, to some extent, a consequence of teaching, although the connection is never as direct as teachers would hope. Teaching may not be translated directly into pupil learning outcomes for a number of reasons. These include the difficulty of matching tasks to pupil capacities, the fact that some pupils spend more time on tasks than others and the fact that pupils misunderstand what they are being asked to learn (Bennett 1989). There is also the evidence (Willis 1977) that some pupils in secondary schools are frequently alienated or disaffected from the learning process. Our evidence is about what the teachers recorded themselves as having spent *their* time on, not the time available to their pupils to study specific subjects. Although there is no doubt a fairly close connection between the two, it is a distinction that needs to be borne in mind throughout this chapter. The connection between teaching and learning should not be taken for granted.

Second, there is a difference between contact time and curriculum time, as can be seen from the way we have defined them in Figure 1.1. Most of the time that teachers spend in contact with pupils is spent teaching them. However, as we have shown in Chapter 3, secondary teachers spend a proportion of time each weekday in contact with pupils when they are working with them but not formally teaching them. The time spent varies, but in our samples it was something over three-quarters of an hour a weekday altogether. There was a close match between the two samples, with Sample 1 spending forty-eight minutes and Sample 2 forty-seven minutes on all such activities.

The main activities of this sort are taking the daily register, participating in assembly, collecting dinner money, supervising pupils at various times in the school day (supervision, registration and assembly) and dealing with individual pupils on matters of discipline or welfare (pastoral). Included in the code for registration is transition, i.e., moving pupils from one place to another within the school, for example from the classroom to the hall for assembly. These activities are not included in our definition of curriculum time, i.e., teaching, but they are included in contact time.

Our approach has two connected advantages. It enables us to take account of times notionally available for teaching but not actually used for it and thus to show the part these occupy in the working day of teachers. Second, it enables us to examine with more precision than would otherwise be the case the time available in practice for the delivery of the curriculum.

TIME SPENT TEACHING: GENERAL FINDINGS

The general findings for our two samples are given in Table 4.1. It can be seen from Table 4.1 that the teachers could record any of four sub-categories of teaching, distinguishing between times when they were teaching their main subject and other subjects, and including testing and National Curriculum assessment when these were carried out during teaching time.

Main subjects were defined for this purpose as subjects that the teachers had studied in higher education for a minimum of two years. Teaching anything else was recorded as 'other

Table 4.1 Time spent teaching

| | Hours per week | | | % of total |
Distribution of time	Sample 1	Sample 2	All teachers	teaching time
Teaching main subject	13.9	15.3	14.0	82
Teaching other subject	2.5	2.4	2.5	15
Teacher assessment	0.4	0.3	0.4	2
Testing	0.8	1.0	0.8	5
Total teaching time	16.9	18.1	17.0	100

subjects', so that a young mathematics graduate who took a couple of lessons of PE, for example, would record the PE as other subject teaching. We also asked teachers to record the occasions when, in lesson time, they were engaged in either testing or National Curriculum assessment. The reason here was that we were aware that some teaching time in secondary schools, especially in the Spring term, is given over to mock examinations and the administration of other tests. We wished to identify this time separately from teaching where this was possible. Also we wanted to identify the time when teachers were carrying out assessment whilst teaching for the National Curriculum, commonly referred to as teacher assessment. The data were collected at a time when no administration of National Curriculum tests (SATs) was occurring, so this was not recorded.

In theory, it would have been possible for teachers to enter two codes together into the same time space. This would be where a teacher was engaged in integrated subject teaching, perhaps as part of a team with Year 7 or 8 pupils. For example, a history graduate might be part of a team teaching an integrated humanities programme covering history, geography, English and RE. Or a physics graduate might be teaching biology as part of a combined science programme. Equally, where teachers were teaching their main subject and, as part of the lesson, administered a test, they could record both activities in the same time space. It is clear from Table 4.1, where the total for the total teaching time is only marginally less (17.0 as against 17.7) than the sum of the component parts, that very little of this simultaneous working occurred. This is in contrast to our evidence (see Campbell and Neill 1994) about primary teachers, where the sum of component parts was almost twice the total time spent teaching, reflecting the common practice of integrated teaching in primary schools.

From Table 4.1 it can be seen that the teachers spent by far the most time teaching their main subject, with fourteen hours (82 per cent) out of the seventeen hours a week spent teaching being concerned with the main subject. In Sample 1, teachers in small schools spent significantly ($p<.01$ linear trend) more time teaching other subjects than teachers in large schools, presumably because small schools have to deploy teachers in more flexible ways. In Sample 2, however, there was more main subject teaching in small schools; the explanation may be the fact that the small schools in that sample were selective schools.

We were able to examine the relationship between what teachers said, on an item on the questionnaire, about the amount of time they spent teaching their main subject and the actual time they recorded. Teachers who said on the questionnaire that they spent more time teaching their main subject actually spent significantly more time doing so ($p < .001$ linear trend). This is one of the many instances where we were able to demonstrate that the teachers were recording in an internally consistent way – that our evidence was reliable. (See Appendix for a further discussion of this point.)

Finally, the substantial amount of time given over to testing, equivalent to about fifty minutes a week, 5 per cent of all teaching time, reflects the emphasis given in secondary schools to preparation for external examinations. The small amount of time given over to teacher assessment for the National Curriculum is partly explained by the fact that some teachers did not teach pupils in Key Stage 3, where such assessment was required. Nonetheless, the amount involved was very small compared to the time spent on such assessment (just under fifty minutes per week) by Key Stage 1 teachers in 1989–90 (see Campbell and Neill 1994). The National Curriculum at Key Stage 1 in 1989–90 was at a broadly comparable implementation phase to the position at Key Stage 3 in 1990/1. Our findings here are similar to those of a survey by HMI (Department of Education and Science 1991a) in which it was reported that, compared to Key Stage 1 teachers, Key Stage 3 teachers were less involved in National Curriculum assessment.

For Sample 1, we had asked the teachers to record their teaching time to each of the Key Stages, and could therefore analyse separately the time devoted to each. In this way we were able to construct a composite picture of the proportion of teaching delivered at each Key Stage by the average teacher. The figures are given in Table 4.2. The composite picture for all our teachers was that they spent 38 per cent of their teaching time with Key Stage 3, 39 per cent with Key Stage 4 and 23 per cent in the stage we call sixth form.

As might be expected, these means, perhaps more than most others in the tables in this book, hide very great variation, since some teachers did no teaching in particular Key Stages. The

Table 4.2 Time spent teaching, by Key
Stage (Sample 1)

Distribution of time	Hours per week	%
Key Stage 3	6.4	38
Key Stage 4	6.6	39
Sixth form	3.95	23
All teaching	16.95	100

minimum and maximum times for each Key Stage illustrated this point clearly. The minimum for each Key Stage was nil, showing that some teachers did no teaching at that stage. The maxima for Key Stage 3, Key Stage 4 and sixth form were 24.3, 18.3 and 24.3 hours respectively.

VARIATIONS IN THE PATTERN OF TEACHING LOADS

We were able to analyse variables associated with differences in teaching loads. This is done below only in respect of Sample 1 because of the small numbers involved in Sample 2, although, where appropriate, we comment on patterns in the latter also.

SALARY STATUS AND TEACHING LOADS

There was a strong negative relationship between salary status and the amount of teaching. This is shown in Table 4.3.

Table 4.3 Time spent teaching, by salary
status (Sample 1)

Salary status	Hours per week teaching
National Standard Scale	18.3
Incentive Allowance 'A'	18.25
Incentive Allowance 'B'	17.9
Incentive Allowance 'C'	18.2
Incentive Allowance 'D'	16.3
Incentive Allowance 'E'	15.0
Deputy head	8.75
Mean	16.9

The point to emphasise here is that, although there was a

significant linear trend (p<.001), there was a clear break or threshold at the point between Incentive Allowance 'C' and 'D'. As can be seen from Table 4.3, for all practical purposes there was little difference in amounts of teaching carried out by National Standard Scale and 'A', 'B' and 'C' allowance holders. The reduction in teaching load starts at the level of 'D' allowances and above, when teachers do less than average amounts of teaching. It is worth adding here that school size, which is to some extent related to the number of higher allowances, did not affect the amount of teaching done.

The other positional variable related to the amount of teaching done was whether or not a teacher had a temporary contract. Those on temporary contracts taught for more time than other teachers. This finding has to be treated with caution in that we believe, as we have suggested in Chapter 2, that some teachers reporting that they had temporary contracts may, in fact, have had temporary allowances.

MAIN SUBJECT TEACHING

The teachers spent a majority of their teaching time, 13.9 hours a week, teaching their main subjects. As can be seen from Table 4.4, this was also related to salary status, as is inevitable given the pattern of teaching shown in Table 4.3.

Table 4.4 also shows the proportion of the teaching time devoted to main subject teaching according to salary status. It is expressed as a percentage of the time spent on all teaching in each salary status. This shows very little variation according to

Table 4.4 Time spent teaching main subject, by salary status (Sample 1)

Salary status	Main subject (hours per week)	% of all teaching
National Standard Scale	15.2	83
Incentive Allowance 'A'	15.1	83
Incentive Allowance 'B'	14.6	82
Incentive Allowance 'C'	14.4	79
Incentive Allowance 'D'	14.0	86
Incentive Allowance 'E'	12.9	86
Deputy head	7.3	83
Mean	13.9	82

Table 4.5 Time spent teaching main subject, by
salary status (Sample 2)

Salary status	Main subject (hours per week)	% of all teaching
National Standard Scale	15.4	83
Incentive Allowance 'A'	16.3	85
Incentive Allowance 'B'	14.3	84
Incentive Allowance 'C'	17.2	91
Mean	15.3	85

salary status, though 'D' and 'E' allowance holders had a small amount more of main subject teaching than other teachers.

In Table 4.5 we show hours and proportions of teaching time given to main subject teaching in Sample 2. Again, the general picture is of over 80 per cent of time spent on main subject teaching, even though there was marginally more time on such teaching overall. The mainland UK titles for allowances are used for comparative purposes. The proportion for 'C' allowance holders needs to be treated with caution since there were only three such teachers.

OTHER SUBJECT TEACHING

Other subject teaching was also related to salary status, but the linear trend was less strong ($p < 0.05$) than for main subject teaching. The higher up the salary scale the less other subject teaching was carried out, again because less teaching of any kind was done by those on the higher scales. Table 4.6 provides the data in respect of Sample 1 both for hours per week and expressed as a percentage of all teaching.

It can be seen from the latter column that, again, there was very little variation, though 'D' and 'E' allowance holders, who carried out more main subject teaching, as has been shown in Table 4.4, carried out less other subject teaching. The pattern of teaching for teachers in these two salary statuses, when the total teaching time is controlled, was thus slightly differentiated from that of all other teachers, including the deputy heads.

In Table 4.7 the time spent on other subject teaching in Sample 2 is shown for comparative purposes. In this sample the teachers on the National Standard Scale spent a greater proportion of their time on other subject teaching, a factor possibly

Table 4.6 Time spent teaching other subjects, by
salary status (Sample 1)

Salary status	Other subjects (hours per week)	% of all teaching
National Standard Scale	2.75	15
Incentive Allowance 'A'	2.7	15
Incentive Allowance 'B'	3.1	17
Incentive Allowance 'C'	3.0	17
Incentive Allowance 'D'	2.0	12
Incentive Allowance 'E'	1.9	13
Deputy head	1.5	17
Mean	2.5	15

associated with teaching at Key Stage 3, and collaborative teaching, as we discuss below.

The other factors associated with other subject teaching were size of school, age of pupils taught and the extent of collaborative teaching. There was slightly more teaching of main subject in the larger schools, and significantly ($p < .001$ linear trend) more other subject teaching in smaller schools. This is because, as we have suggested earlier, the smaller schools do not have the same range of staff as larger schools and therefore can deploy them less as teachers of their main subject only. In smaller schools teachers need to be more flexible in what they teach.

The majority of teachers, 237 out of the 348, had no time when they were working alongside another teacher. The remainder spent some time teaching with another teacher in their class – i.e., in some form of team teaching or collaborative teaching. This variable was positively and strongly ($p < .001$ linear trend)

Table 4.7 Time spent teaching other subjects, by
salary status (Sample 2)

Salary status	Other subjects (hours per week)	% of all teaching
National Standard Scale	3.1	17
Incentive Allowance 'A'	2.3	12
Incentive Allowance 'B'	2.4	14
Incentive Allowance 'C'	1.3	7
Mean	2.4	13

associated with other subject teaching. Those who spent more time with a colleague in their class carried out more other subject teaching. This suggests that these teachers are more often engaged in some form of integrated thematic work in which they teach subjects for which they have relatively little academic background. It is unclear whether they engage in such teaching as a deliberate policy or whether it is forced upon them by virtue of the size of school in which they are teaching.

The picture is further complicated by the fact that the amount of teaching at Key Stage 3 was strongly ($p<.001$ linear trend) and positively associated with the amount of time spent with a colleague in the class. Teaching at sixth-form level, on the other hand, was strongly ($p<.001$ linear trend) and negatively associated with collaborative teaching.

What emerges, therefore, is a complex picture of other subject teaching; it is carried out by a substantial minority of teachers, more often working in small schools, and is mainly carried out with the younger pupils in collaborative team teaching arrangements, which probably help teachers deal with the fact that they are teaching material which is different from their main subject.

SEX OF TEACHERS AND TEACHING LOADS

We have already shown that there was no statistical difference between the total workloads of men and women teachers in Sample 1. There was also no statistically significant difference between the amount of overall teaching carried out by men ($n=151$) and women ($n=187$) teachers, although the men taught for slightly less time – 16.5 hours per week against the women's 17.1 hours. The explanation is probably due to the fact that rather more men were in higher salary status positions and, as the multiple regression analysis showed, salary status was the best predictor of time spent teaching, with high status being associated with low amounts of teaching.

However, there was a difference in the amount of teaching carried out with younger pupils. Female teachers did significantly ($p<.01$ analysis of variance) more teaching at Key Stage 3. They taught Key Stage 3 pupils for 6.5 hours a week compared to the men's 5.25 hours. As might be expected, the picture at sixth-form level was reversed, with women doing significantly ($p<.05$ analysis of variance) less of such teaching, and men doing more. The men taught sixth-form students for 4.4 hours per week compared to the women's 3.25 hours. There was no difference between the sexes in respect of amounts of teaching at Key Stage 4. The multiple regression analysis showed the amount of Key Stage 3 teaching was negatively related to salary status and non-contact time, and positively related to collaborative teaching. Sixth-form teaching was negatively related to collaborative teaching and positively related to time on main subjects. Again, in both stages, salary status was the best predictor of the time spent teaching.

SIZES OF CLASSES TAUGHT

The teachers were asked to record the size of the classes they taught. The figure they recorded for this purpose was the number of pupils in the class they were teaching at any particular time rather than the number of pupils registered. The figure thus is equivalent to that used by the DES and referred to in its annual statistics as size of class 'as taught'. Table 4.8 gives the figures, broken down by Key Stage, for Sample 1.

Table 4.8 shows the differences in class size by Key Stage, with smaller class sizes as the pupils get older. The figures in this table are very similar to those in the 1990 Annual Statistics from the DES (Department of Education and Science 1990b), except that the class size at sixth-form level is larger in our sample. This is possibly explained by the fact that some of the teachers in our sample were working in tertiary colleges/FE colleges where the class size tends to be larger than that operating in the conventional sixth form.

The data for Sample 2 were similar, as can be seen from Table 4.9, although the sixth-form figure was more typical of sixth-form

Table 4.8 Mean size of class taught, by Key Stage (Sample 1)

Key Stage	Class size
Key Stage 3	22
Key Stage 4	18
Sixth form	11
Mean class size	18

Table 4.9 Mean size of class
taught, by Key Stage (Sample 2)

Key Stage	Class size
Key Stage 3	25
Key Stage 4	17
Sixth form	5
Mean class size	18

teaching groups nationally. This is because in Sample 2 the sixth forms were more conventional grammar school groups.

TEACHER PRODUCTIVITY

We were able to compute a measure of teacher 'productivity' from the data on class size. We defined productivity in the limited sense of the number of pupils taught per teacher, multiplied by the amount of time they were taught at each Key Stage. This is expressed as an index of the number of pupil minutes taught per day. We were not in any sense measuring the quality of teaching, which might improve as class size fell, but were simply measuring quantity. As might be expected, productivity in this limited sense decreased as the age of pupils increased. The figures are given in Table 4.10 for Sample 1.

Table 4.10 Teacher productivity,
by Key Stage (Sample 1)

Key Stage	Pupil minutes taught per day
Key Stage 3	1,956
Key Stage 4	1,586
Sixth form	883

Whatever its defects as a measure, the teacher productivity index provides the basis for analysing differences in workload that are not available from a simple consideration of the amount of time spent teaching. For example, we have shown that women teach significantly more at Key Stage 3 than men, whilst the latter teach more at sixth-form level. In terms of our index of productivity, therefore, the female teachers were more productive than the male teachers. We were also able to show that teachers on the National Standard Scale taught significantly more at Key Stage 3, even when sex is controlled for. Thus it could also be argued that the lower-paid teachers were more productive, by our definition.

MATCH OF BACKGROUND TO TEACHING DUTIES

A number of items on the questionnaire allowed us to obtain subjective and objective measures of the extent to which the teachers' academic backgrounds were matched to their teaching duties. The full details have been provided in Chapter 2. In order to provide us with a relatively objective definition of match in this respect, they were asked to record the main subjects that they had studied for at least two years in higher education, and to name only two subjects at most. In the event, the 348 teachers in Sample 1 named 481 subjects, with the core subjects of the National Curriculum taking up more than half of these responses (mathematics 77; science 140; English 43). The teachers were then asked to say how much time to the nearest hour they spent teaching the subjects they had named as their main subjects. Table 4.11 gives the distribution across the time categories for Sample 1.

These figures need to be treated with some caution since they have to be considered alongside the evidence from the Records of Teacher Time provided earlier in this chapter (Table 4.1) that the teachers spent, on average, 16.9 hours a week teaching, and that teachers on higher salary statuses did relatively small amounts of teaching. Nevertheless, for whatever reasons, the data in Table 4.11, derived from the questionnaire responses, show that nearly one in five of the teachers reported that they were teaching their main subjects for fewer than ten hours a week.

Table 4.11 Time spent teaching main subjects

Hours per week	Number of teachers	% teachers
5 or less	36	10
5 – 10	28	8
10 – 15	75	22
15 – 20	139	40
Over 20	70	20
Total	348	100

Table 4.12 Perceptions of match of academic background to current teaching

Academic background	Number of teachers	% teachers
Well matched	62	18
Well matched to most	141	41
Well matched to only half	53	15
Well matched to only a small amount	87	25
Don't know	5	2
Total	348	100

Teachers were also asked how far they considered that their academic background was well matched to their current teaching duties. This was intended to provide a subjective view of the match between main subjects and teaching, to complement the objective one above. The data for Sample 1 are given in Tables 4.12–4.16.

It can be seen that 40 per cent of the teachers thought that their academic background was well matched to no more than half or a small amount of the teaching they were required to carry out. This subjective judgement is different from the picture obtained by using the objective measure above. It suggests a poorer match in teachers' perceptions than would be arrived at from considering their qualifications only.

Finally, we asked the teachers about how well they thought their academic backgrounds had prepared them for the teaching of the foundation subjects of the National Curriculum in Years 7 –11, i.e., in Key Stages 3 and 4. Teachers were asked which of the foundation subjects they were teaching in Years 7–11. Of the 348 teachers 299 replied, naming 386 subjects. In this way we excluded those teachers who were not teaching in Years 7–11 and who might not have had a good basis for arriving at a judgement about this matter. The figures are given in Table 4.13.

We also asked the teachers for their subjective judgement about how well they considered their academic background had prepared them for such teaching. Table 4.14 shows the numbers of teachers judging their training to be adequate.

It can be seen from Table 4.14 that fewer subjects were named overall than in Table 4.13. This suggests that the general picture is that the teachers are, to some extent, teaching subjects that

Table 4.13 Perceptions of match of academic background to National Curriculum foundation subjects

Subject	Number of responses	% responses
Mathematics	79	21
English	44	11
Science	79	21
Technology	36	9
History	38	10
Geography	40	10
Modern languages	37	10
Music	7	2
Art	10	3
PE	16	4
Total	386	100

Table 4.14 Teachers perceiving their training to be adequate for teaching National Curriculum foundation subjects

Subject	Number of responses	% responses
Mathematics	71	22
English	38	12
Welsh	1	<1
Science	69	21
Technology	20	6
History	37	11
Geography	33	10
Modern languages	32	10
Music	6	2
Art	6	2
PE	11	3
Total	324	100

they feel inadequately prepared to teach. In addition, the differences between subjects reveal that those teaching technology see themselves as less well prepared than those teaching other subjects, with only twenty of the thirty-six teachers involved seeing themselves as adequately prepared.

We can now summarise the position about the match between academic background and teaching duties by combining the data from Tables 4.11–4.14 into the following table, Table 4.15.

Table 4.15 Subject match as measured by different criteria

Match	% of teachers with poor match
(1) Objective (all teaching)	18
(2) Subjective (all teaching)	40
(3) Subjective (all Years 7–11) (see Table 4.16)	3–44

Table 4.16 Teachers perceiving their backgrounds as poorly matched to National Curriculum teaching

Subject	Numbers teaching	Numbers reporting	% poorly matched
Technology	36	20	44
Art	10	6	40
PE	16	11	31
Geography	40	33	18
English	44	38	14
Music	7	6	14
Modern languages	37	32	14
Science	79	69	13
Mathematics	79	71	10
History	38	37	3

On this table 'poor match' is defined as follows: in row (1), fewer than ten hours of all teaching; in row (2), less than half of all teaching; in row (3), not adequately prepared by academic background.

In respect of the foundation subjects up to Year 11, there was considerable variation according to the subject, as is indicated in row (3). The proportion of teachers who were teaching foundation subjects, but did not feel adequately prepared by either their academic background or by subsequent re-training, was as given in Table 4.16. The percentages are created from the numbers of teachers teaching a subject and the numbers reporting themselves as adequately prepared (i.e., from Tables 4.13 and 4.14 above).

The policy and management issues arising from these findings are discussed in Chapter 8.

SUMMARY

The teachers spent seventeen hours a week teaching, for fourteen of which they were teaching a subject they defined as one of the main subjects in which they were qualified. For two-and-a-half hours they taught subjects in which they were unqualified. The rest of their teaching time was taken up with testing and assessment. Those on higher salary scales taught less than those on lower scales. Average class size varied by Key Stage, with Key Stage 3 classes at twenty-two pupils, Key Stage 4 at eighteen pupils and 16–19 classes at eleven students. Women taught Key Stage 3 classes more often than men. Using an index of teacher productivity we showed that female teachers were more productive than male teachers, and teachers on National Standard Scale were more productive than others. Forty per cent of the teachers thought that up to half of their teaching was not well matched to their academic background, and poor match varied according to subject, with technology being the poorest match.

5

PREPARATION AND PROFESSIONAL DEVELOPMENT

In this chapter we examine the data for both samples on preparation and on professional development activities, both separately and in combination. We divided preparation into three sub-categories, viz., lesson planning; marking and recording; and organising learning resources. In this chapter and elsewhere we use the word preparation to refer to the overall category, not the sub-category of lesson planning which it sometimes means in everyday usage.

We divided professional development into five sub-categories, viz., training courses/conferences; travel to training courses/conferences; non-pupil days ('Baker' days); meetings, whether formal or informal; and reading professional journals, magazines, National Curriculum documents, etc.

We have treated the two categories in combination because the two kinds of activity can be thought of as directly or indirectly contributing to, or feeding into, the work of teaching pupils. Preparation directly feeds into lessons since it involves planning lessons or marking and recording pupils' work. Professional development feeds in much less directly, since it may involve training for particular aspects of the curriculum, management, assessment or meetings in which the work of the school, the department or individual pupils is discussed.

However, preparation has also been treated separately from professional development. Our reasons are these: the two activities are thought of as different in the everyday discourse of teachers; they have been treated differently in previous studies; and, while all preparation time feeds into teaching, some aspects of professional development (e.g., some time spent in meetings) may be only distantly, if at all, related to classroom performance.

One other introductory point should be made about preparation. It is the area of teachers' work most obviously subject to the exercise of discretion by individual teachers. The amount of time they spend upon lesson planning, marking and organising resources is, to a large extent, up to them. Obviously the matter is not entirely unconstrained; it may be affected by such aspects of their working conditions as how many hours a week they teach, how large their classes are and how much marking has to feed into officially required reports. Nonetheless, when these matters have been allowed for, the amount of time that teachers devote to preparation is mainly dependent on their individual sense of professional obligation – on what time is needed to do the job properly according to their perceptions of professional standards. Some aspects of professional development, e.g., voluntarily attending training courses or conferences, likewise may be seen as dependent on perceptions of professionalism. In short, preparation and, to a lesser extent, professional development, are the parts of the teachers' job most subject to 'conscientiousness' because they fall, more often than other categories of work, into non-directed time. This issue is discussed more fully in Chapter 10.

TIME ON PREPARATION AND PROFESSIONAL DEVELOPMENT COMBINED

Table 5.1 shows the time spent on all preparation and professional development combined, by both samples, in hours per week. The data are broken down according to whether the time was spent during the weekdays or at weekends.

It can be seen from Table 5.1 that the time spent was similar across the two samples, as was the distribution of time across

Table 5.1 Time spent on preparation and professional development combined: weekdays and weekends

Sample	Hours per week		
	Weekdays	*Weekends*	*Total*
Sample 1	14.1	4.0	18.1
Sample 2	13.8	4.0	17.8
All teachers	14.1	4.0	18.1

weekdays and weekends. Two further points should be made. First, the total time on preparation and professional development was a third of the teachers' total working time and more than the time spent teaching (seventeen hours a week), as we have shown in Chapter 3. Second, the daily time is substantial – 2.8 hours a day during the week and two hours per day at weekends. It could be argued, therefore, that in considering the management of teachers' time, head teachers should assume that for every hour of teaching allocated there is more than another hour of preparation or professional development involved for the average teacher.

A further analysis of preparation and professional development time concerns time spent on and off school premises. The data are given in Table 5.2.

Two points may be drawn from Table 5.2. First, as with the distribution in Table 5.1, the divisions of time are broadly similar for the two samples. Second, the time spent off school premises is, as might be expected, greater than the time spent on school premises. The main reason for this, as we shall see later in this chapter, is that when the combined time is analysed separately for time on preparation and professional development, the majority of time was spent in preparation, and most preparation was done at home.

When we analysed the time on preparation and professional development combined according to other variables, for example, by salary status or sex or type of school, we found no statistical differences. This is because the combination of the two categories obscured many differences in the time spent on the individual categories since they are alternative uses of working time outside teaching hours. It is to the analysis of the two categories separately that we now turn.

Table 5.2 Time spent on preparation and professional development combined: on and off school premises

	Hours per week		
Sample	On school premises	Off school premises	Total
Sample 1	8.0	10.1	18.1
Sample 2	7.4	10.4	17.8
All teachers	7.9	10.1	18.0

PREPARATION

The time spent on preparation and the three sub-categories that comprise it in our coding system are given for both samples in Table 5.3.

Table 5.3 Time spent on preparation and sub-categories

Category	Hours per week		
	Sample 1	Sample 2	All teachers
Lesson planning	5.8	6.2	5.8
Marking/recording	6.8	8.5	7.0
Organising resources	1.2	1.4	1.2
All preparation	12.9	15.3	13.1

Three points emerge from Table 5.3. First, there is broad similarity of time distribution across the sub-categories by two samples. (There was proportionately more marking and less planning in Sample 2, but the differences were not statistically significant.) Second, the total time is smaller than the sum of the sub-categories since, for some of the time, teachers were engaged in two sub-categories simultaneously. They could be using their marking of pupils' work as the first stage of their planning, or they could be planning lessons and organising the relevant resources simultaneously. The amount of overlap, however, is relatively small since the sum of the sub-categories is only 0.9 hours greater than the total time. Third, the common stereotype of the secondary teacher with very large amounts of marking but fairly small amounts of lesson planning is challenged by these data. These teachers spent almost as much time on planning lessons as on marking/recording. If organising resources is included as lesson planning, they spent as much time on planning as on marking and recording.

A further point is that preparation time was equivalent to 76 per cent of the time spent teaching. From this we can infer that for every hour of teaching that the average teacher is allocated, over three-quarters of an hour further will have to be spent on preparation. Teaching and preparation together constituted thirty hours a week on average, 55 per cent of the total time spent on work.

We were able to show the proportions of time spent on

Table 5.4 Time spent on preparation and sub-categories: weekdays and weekends

| | Hours per week | | | | | |
| | Sample 1 | | Sample 2 | | All teachers | |
Category	Week-days	Week-ends	Week-days	Week-ends	Week-days	Week-ends
Lesson planning	4.4	1.4	4.6	1.6	4.4	1.4
Marking/recording	5.1	1.7	6.6	1.9	5.2	1.7
Organising resources	0.9	0.2	1.2	0.2	0.9	0.2
All preparation	9.7	3.2	11.8	3.5	9.9	3.2

Table 5.5 Time spent on preparation and sub-categories: on and off school premises

| | Hours per week | | | | | |
| | Sample 1 | | Sample 2 | | All teachers | |
Category	On	Off	On	Off	On	Off
Lesson planning	2.7	3.2	2.9	3.3	2.7	3.2
Marking/recording	2.5	4.3	3.0	5.5	2.8	4.4
Organising resources	0.7	0.4	0.9	0.5	0.7	0.4
All preparation	5.4	7.5	6.3	9.0	5.5	7.6

preparation on and off school premises and on weekdays and at weekends. These are given in Table 5.4 and Table 5.5.

It can be seen from these two tables, as with the previous ones in this chapter, that there is broad similarity in the patterning of the time across the sub-categories in the two samples. The proportions of time spent on and off school premises, and on weekdays and at weekends, were not statistically significantly different for the two samples.

Three other points can be drawn out from these two tables. First, almost a quarter of preparation time occurred at weekends and, as might be expected, very little of this was concerned with organising resources. Most of this activity has to be done during the week and on school premises, since much of it is concerned with organising materials and equipment in science or language laboratories or other school-based resources. Second, although most of the marking was done during the week, a considerable proportion (63 per cent) was undertaken at home. Teachers still take their marking home with them. Third, the pattern for

Table 5.6 Minimum and maximum times for aspects of preparation

Category	Hours per week		
	Mean	Minimum	Maximum
All preparation	12.8	0	37.5
All preparation (weekdays)	9.7	0	28.6
All preparation (weekends)	3.2	0	16.0
Lesson planning	5.8	0	22.9
Marking/recording	6.8	0	26.8
Organising resources	1.2	0	15.1
All preparation (on premises)	5.4	0	22.3
All preparation (off premises)	7.5	0	28.5

lesson planning, although similar to that for marking in distribution across weekdays/weekends, differed in that relatively less planning was done off school premises (55 per cent). This suggests that lesson planning, more than marking, was carried out in non-contact time during the school day.

It should be said that these means disguised great variation amongst individuals. The minima and maxima for aspects of preparation for Sample 1 are given in Table 5.6, and reveal the range of differences in time on preparation.

The explanation for these differences is threefold. First, in any one week a teacher may be working in what is for him/her an untypical way. For example, in the last week of term there may be less preparation than in the first week of term. Equally, in the weeks when mock GCSE examinations were done by pupils, there would be unusually heavy marking loads for the teachers concerned. We do not know how typical the recorded week was for the individual doing the recording.

Second, some teachers on the higher salary scales did much less teaching than others, and we would expect that preparation would vary according to the amount of teaching in any overall workload. The variation is in this respect expected.

Third, the differences reflect something of the unstable pattern of teachers' work; some weeks they have to do more of one aspect, e.g., preparation, whilst in others they do more of another, e.g., professional development. It is probably the case that this instability in patterning of work shows up more in aspects of preparation than in other areas because of the intensive but spasmodic role that examinations and testing take in the work of secondary school teachers.

Preparation by Key Stage

We were able to calculate the amount of time on preparation according to the age of pupils being taught in one of three Key Stages, namely Key Stage 3 (Years 7–9 of the National Curriculum); Key Stage 4 (Years 10–11); and sixth form (the post-statutory years). The data here relate to total preparation and are not disaggregated into sub-categories. The figures are given in Table 5.7.

Table 5.7 Mean preparation time by Key Stage (Sample 1)

	Hours per week on preparation	
Key Stage	*Sample 1*	*Sample 2*
Key Stage 3	3.7	4.3
Key Stage 4	4.2	6.3
Sixth form	2.7	3.2
Not specified/other	2.0	1.5

It is important to point out that the mean hours per week are for all teachers and are not for only those teachers who spent time on preparation for a particular Key Stage. Since not all teachers worked in all three stages, and some teachers worked in only one, the means, although an accurate measure of all teachers' distribution of time, are slightly misleading.

There are two ways to examine the relationship of preparation time to teaching time at each Key Stage; for this examination we used data from Sample 1 teachers. The first way is to set the mean preparation time for the 348 teachers against the proportion of teaching time typically spent at each Key Stage. This evidence has been provided in Table 4.2 in the previous chapter. Ignoring the preparation time not specified for a particular Key Stage, we can translate the preparation hours in Table 5.7 into percentages. Put together, these two sets of data would be as in Table 5.8.

Thus, the evidence in Table 5.8 suggests that the balance of preparation to teaching is roughly proportionate, with slightly less preparation at Key Stage 3 and slightly more at sixth-form level than is strictly proportionate. However, the above analysis omits any consideration of class size which, in theory, ought to affect the time spent on marking and recording results. For this

Table 5.8 Proportion of time spent on
teaching and preparation at each Key
Stage

Key Stage	% teaching	% preparation
Key Stage 3	38	35
Key Stage 4	39	40
Sixth form	23	26

Table 5.9 Weekly preparation time per pupil, by Key Stage

		Hours per week	
Sample	Class size	Preparation time	Preparation time per pupil
Sample 1:			
Key Stage 3	22	3.7	0.16
Key Stage 4	18	4.2	0.23
Sixth form	11	2.7	0.25
Sample 2:			
Key Stage 3	25	4.3	0.17
Key Stage 4	17	6.3	0.37
Sixth form	5	3.2	0.64

purpose a further calculation was carried out to show the mean
preparation time per pupil for the Key Stages shown above. This
was done by dividing the time spent on preparation by the size
of teaching group, which has been provided in Chapter 4, page
79. This is shown, for both samples, in Table 5.9.

For the reasons indicated in the previous paragraph, the
relation of the calculation of preparation time to teaching and to
class size is a little crude and, if anything, gives a picture of the
time spent at each Key Stage that is less differentiated than in
reality. But, even so, the broad picture is consistent from both
perspectives. The older the pupils the less economic the preparation time, or the more preparation time is called for by the
nature of the teaching. Table 5.9 shows that if weekly preparation time is divided by the average class size in a Key Stage, the
preparation time per pupil per week increases with the age of
the pupils. In Sample 2, where sixth-form groups were smallest,
preparation time per pupil was much the largest. From the point
of view of the individual pupil, more teacher time on preparation becomes available with smaller classes; from the point of
view of the school as an institution, teacher preparation time is

more economic with large classes. At one level this is banal; individuals in large classes cannot expect large amounts of preparation. However, if the large per capita preparation time is to some extent associated with the work of examinations and testing at Key Stage 4 and sixth form, as was likely in 1991, we might expect preparation time at Key Stage 3 to increase significantly as, after 1993, national testing in the foundation subjects comes progressively on-stream at Key Stage 3, even under modified arrangements proposed by the Dearing review (National Curriculum Council/SEAC 1993).

Variation in preparation

We were able to examine variation related to aspects of the questionnaire, such as the professional biographies of the teachers, their working conditions and their perceptions of time on work. Because of the small numbers involved in Sample 2, the relationships that are discussed below are for Sample 1 only.

Conscientiousness

There was a strong positive ($p<.001$ linear trend) statistical association between the amount of their own, non-directed time that teachers thought it was reasonable for them to be expected to spend on work and the time they spent on preparation. This association held for preparation overall, during the weekdays but not weekends, off school premises but not on them. Within the sub-categories conscientiousness was associated positively with time spent on lesson planning ($p<.05$ linear trend), especially on school premises, and on organising resources ($p<.05$ linear trend), especially on school premises. Conscientiousness, therefore, had an effect on the amount of time spent on lesson planning and organising resources, but not on marking. We discuss the conscientiousness thesis in Chapter 10 but would infer from the statistical associations that it influences those aspects of preparation where individual discretion comes into greater play. The amount of time spent on marking/recording is logically more dependent on factors such as the amount of teaching and assignments set; but lesson planning and organising resources, whilst obviously affected by the amount of teaching done, is influenced more by teachers' conscientiousness.

Salary status

There was a strong (p<.01 linear trend) negative correlation between salary status and amount of time spent on preparation; the higher the salary status the less the preparation time. This is to be expected given that, as we have shown in Chapter 4, teachers on higher salary statuses teach less. However, the picture is less obvious than might be predicted from Table 4.3 in Chapter 4. Scrutiny of the detailed data shows that the main source of difference in amounts of time spent on preparation was due to the deputy heads, who spent less than an hour a day compared to the average of nearly two hours. 'D' and 'E' allowance holders, on the other hand, spent somewhat more time on preparation than 'C' and 'B' allowance holders, despite doing less teaching than them.

The statistical relationship between salary status and preparation was particularly marked for preparation during the weekdays (p<.001 linear trend) and on school premises (p<.001 linear trend). It was particularly strong for lesson planning (p<.001 linear trend), as might be expected given the smaller amounts of teaching done by deputies, but not for marking or organising resources where the relationship was not significant statistically.

The picture, therefore, is more complex than might be thought from considering the amount of teaching done, since there was not a direct connection between amounts of teaching and amounts of preparation, except for the deputies. Even they spent rather similar amounts of time on marking and organising resources to those spent by other teachers. If we leave deputies out of consideration, there seems only a tenuous relationship between time spent teaching overall (as opposed to teaching differentiated by Key Stage) and time spent on preparation. We conclude from this that the explanation associated with conscientiousness above is supported. Everyone has to do some preparation but, after the minimum has been done, conscientiousness, rather than the amount of teaching that has to be prepared for, comes into play.

Main subject teaching and academic match

We mean by 'main subject teaching' the amount of time spent teaching subjects identified by the teachers as those they had studied for at least two years in higher education. By 'academic match' we mean the extent to which the teachers perceived that the academic background obtained from their initial training was well matched to current teaching duties. We are thus taking further the analysis of match raised in Chapter 4.

There was a positive and consistent pattern of statistical association between main subject teaching and preparation, with teachers who spent more time teaching their main subject(s) spending more time on preparation. This was true for all preparation ($p<.001$ linear trend), on weekdays ($p<.001$ linear trend), for weekends ($p<.01$ linear trend), on school premises ($p<.01$ linear trend) and off them ($p<.001$ linear trend). There was also a strong association between main subject teaching and time on two sub-categories of preparation. These were lesson planning ($p<.001$ linear trend), whether on weekdays ($p<.01$ linear trend) or at weekends ($p<.001$ linear trend), on school premises ($p<.05$ linear trend) or off them ($p<.001$ linear trend); and marking/recording ($p<.001$ linear trend), on weekdays ($p<.001$ linear trend), on school premises ($p<.01$ linear trend) and off them ($p<.05$ linear trend). There was no relationship between main subject teaching and the third sub-category, organising resources.

The strength and consistency of these associations are dramatic, and can be explained only partly by the obvious fact that those doing more main subject teaching will be doing more teaching overall and, therefore, will have to do more preparation. We have shown above that, except for deputy heads, this explanation did not hold true. It might be expected that those teachers who spend more time teaching subjects that are not their main subject would need to spend more time on preparation, or at least on lesson planning, to make up for the relative lack of knowledge. The evidence does not support this idea. On the contrary, it looks as though teachers spend more time on preparation, especially on lesson planning and marking, when the preparation is in the field in which they have specialised. It may be that commitment to one's subject means also commitment to prepare more for teaching it.

There was support for this interpretation from the data on the perceived match of academic background to current teaching duties. Those teachers who saw their academic background as well matched to all their teaching spent more time on preparation than other teachers, although the difference was not statistically significant. However, when preparation for sixth-form teaching alone was considered, the difference was statistically significant (p<.05 linear trend). There was also a statistically significant difference (p<.05 linear trend) in relation to lesson planning, with those seeing their background as being well matched to their teaching spending longer on lesson planning generally, especially at weekends and off school premises. No such trends were evident in relation to marking or organising resources. The explanation we have made, drawing on good match, needs to be qualified by the realities of school life. Some teaching of other subjects would be 'covering' for absent colleagues, often at short notice and sometimes with work set and marked by the regular teacher. This would necessarily mean less preparation for the covering teacher.

Temporary contracts and allowances

Our evidence showed that some teachers were on fixed-term contracts and others had allowances which were temporary; for example, they might be acting head of department during the absence of the allowance holder on secondment, or through illness or because of an unfilled vacancy. Six per cent of teachers reported themselves as holding a temporary allowance whilst 27 per cent said they were on a fixed-term contract. Over one in four teachers considering themselves to be on a fixed-term contract seems very high, and it may be that some of the respondents had read 'fixed-term contract' to mean 'temporary allowance'. On the other hand, the explanation for the large number reporting fixed-term contracts might lie in the awareness amongst a union membership that, technically speaking, all contracts have a fixed term because they can be terminated with three months' notice for good cause. Whatever the reason, it means that the data relating to fixed-term contracts need to be treated with some caution.

Those reporting themselves on fixed-term contracts spent significantly (p<.01 analysis of variance) more time on preparation than other teachers overall. On weekdays, at weekends and off school premises the difference was particularly marked whereas, although there was a slight difference in preparation on school premises, it did not reach statistical significance. The relationship obtained for Key Stage 3 and 4 preparation but not at sixth-form level, and for marking but not for lesson planning or organising resources.

Teachers on temporary allowances, however, showed a different pattern. They did significantly ($p < .05$ analysis of variance) more organising of learning resources off school premises and at weekends.

Despite acknowledging the problematic nature of the data, mentioned earlier, we infer from the data relating to both the above groups of teachers that there is another, less romantic, strand in teacher motivation to spend long hours on preparation than the 'conscientiousness' we referred to earlier. Those whose current status is temporary, or is seen by them as temporary in some sense, may be putting in the longer hours on preparation out of a desire to demonstrate that they should be, or a fear that they will not be, made permanent. It is also the case that temporary status brings with it some teaching tasks and responsibilities that are new to the individual, and will therefore require more preparation initially.

PROFESSIONAL DEVELOPMENT

The category of professional development incorporated five sub-categories, viz., attendance at courses and conferences; travel to courses and conferences; participation in non-pupil days; meetings, both formal and informal; and reading of professional journals and magazines. The data are presented in Table 5.10, for both samples.

The main point to note about Table 5.10 is that meetings took up almost half of professional development time. As we have

Table 5.10 Time spent on professional development

	Hours per week		
Activity	Sample 1	Sample 2	All
Courses/conferences	1.2	0.2	1.1
Travel	0.7	0.2	0.7
Non-pupil days	0.2	0.0	0.2
Meetings	2.5	1.3	2.4
Reading	0.9	0.9	0.9
All professional development	5.4	2.6	5.1

pointed out earlier (p. 62), whether this time should be seen as entirely concerned with professional development is problematic. Some of it would be spent in meetings concerned with developing the curriculum, but other time in this sub-category would be spent in staff and department meetings concerned with routines. Where this was the case the time would be more appropriately allocated to administration. The difficulty here is that many meetings are not purely of one category; they comprise a mix of administrative and staff development activities. A departmental meeting might include discussion of the advantages of purchasing a new set of textbooks and timetabling matters on the one agenda. In this chapter we have assumed that all time in meetings should be counted as spent on professional development activities. Alternative assumptions have been illustrated in Chapter 3.

The second point about the figures in Table 5.10 is that, as elsewhere, the means disguise very great variation. For Sample 1, the minimum hours for the overall category and for each sub-category were zero. The maximum hours are shown in Table 5.11.

Thus, for some teachers in a particular week, no time at all was spent on any professional development. They did not go on any courses, had no non-pupil days, managed to avoid meetings and read nothing. Others spent very long hours travelling to and attending conferences, presumably involving an overnight stay, or spent more than the conventionally required six hours on a non-pupil day, or spent very long hours in meetings or devoted a long time to reading of a professional kind. It should be said that the maxima and minima in each sub-category refer to different individuals.

Table 5.11 Maximum times spent on professional development

Category	Hours per week
Courses/conferences	19.6
Travel	18.2
Non-pupil days	7.6
Meetings	17.6
Reading	11.2
All professional development	30.7

For professional development overall, the proportions of time spent on and off school premises, and whether it was spent at weekends or on weekdays, are given in Table 5.12. It can be seen that most professional development took place during the week and that it was distributed equally between time on and off school premises.

Table 5.13 shows the distribution of time on each sub-category according to whether it was spent during the week or at weekends. The figures refer to Sample 1 only in the following tables because of the small numbers and small amount of time on the first three sub-categories in Sample 2.

The distribution of time on the sub-categories of professional development according to whether it is spent on or off school premises is given in Table 5.14, again for Sample 1 only. It can be seen that the overall time was distributed equally between time on and off school premises. However, nearly all meetings occurred on school premises and nearly all reading occurred off them.

Table 5.12 Time spent on professional development: weekdays and weekends, on and off school premises

| | Hours per week | | |
Time or location	Sample 1	Sample 2	All
Weekdays	4.5	2.1	4.3
Weekends	0.8	0.5	0.8
On school premises	2.7	1.2	2.6
Off school premises	2.7	1.4	2.6
All professional development	5.4	2.6	5.1

Table 5.13 Time spent on sub-categories of professional development: weekdays and weekends

| | Sample 1, hours per week | |
Category	Weekdays	Weekends
Courses	0.9	0.3
Travel	0.5	0.2
Non-pupil days	0.2	0.0
Meetings	2.4	0.1
Reading	0.6	0.3
All professional development	4.6	0.9

100

Table 5.14 Time spent on sub-categories of professional
development: on and off school premises

Category	Sample 1, hours per week	
	On school premises	Off school premises
Courses	0.2	1.0
Travel	0.0	0.7
Non-pupil days	0.2	0.0
Meetings	2.1	0.4
Reading	0.2	0.7
All professional development	2.7	2.7

In-service training

We wished to show the amount of time spent by teachers
directly on in-service training, as opposed to the broader category
of professional development. For this purpose we aggregated
time spent on courses, travel to courses and non-pupil days.
The figures for these sub-categories combined are given in Table
5.15.

Table 5.15 Time spent on courses,
travel and non-pupil days

Time	Sample 1 (hours per week)
Weekdays	1.6
Weekends	0.5
Total	2.1

Thus, just over two hours a week of the teachers' time was
spent on in-service training. This is equivalent to 4 per cent of
the teachers' overall time on work. If travelling time (0.7 hours
per week) is excluded from the calculation, the percentage of
teachers' total time on work given over to in-service training was
just over 2 per cent.

In-service training for Key Stage 3

We had asked the teachers to identify in their records when they
were receiving in-service training for Key Stage 3 of the National
Curriculum. This was to obtain some measure of the extent of

training for the new demands placed upon teachers by the introduction of the core subjects of mathematics and science (from Autumn 1989) and English (from Autumn 1990). The mean time spent by the 348 teachers was 0.25 hours a week, equivalent to two minutes a day. This is a little misleading since only 205 teachers were involved in teaching at Key Stage 3. These teachers averaged 0.4 hours per week on Key Stage 3 training, equivalent to 3.5 minutes per day.

Variation in professional development

There was no difference in time spent on all professional development between men and women. However, women spent significantly ($p<.05$ analysis of variance) more time, just over an hour compared to half an hour, on all professional development at weekends than men did. Professional development at weekends comprised mainly courses, travel to courses and reading, as we have shown in Table 5.14. We infer that the explanation is that women can fit in-service training more easily into weekends than at other times when family pressures may inhibit their participation. In-service training at weekends can be planned for more easily than school-based training or training in 'twilight' hours, when conventional child-care or assistance from husbands/partners is less readily available.

This interpretation is supported by other data in Tables 5.13 and 5.14. Meetings almost never occurred at weekends, but some small amounts of time in meetings (0.4 hours per week) were spent off school premises during weekdays. Men spent significantly ($p<.05$ analysis of variance) more time in these weekday out-of-school meetings than women did. This would follow from our explanation above.

Younger and less experienced teachers spent less time on in-service training (courses, travel to courses, and non-pupil days combined) ($p<.01$ linear trend). This would follow from the adoption of a cascade model by central and local government as the dominant approach to in-service training. In cascade models, a member of staff, usually a more experienced or senior member, is trained on a course with the intention that upon return to school he/she will disseminate what has been learned on the course to other members of staff. However, the picture is complex since salary status was not related to time on in-service training defined in this way. An alternative would be that younger teachers are less 'professional' and committed in this way, i.e., that the reforms rely on old-fashioned commitment. A more jaundiced view of professionalism might lead to the interpretation that young teachers have more interesting things to do with their lives than to go on in-service training sessions, whilst older teachers do not.

Meetings and salary status

There was a strong trend (p<.001 linear trend) for those on higher salary statuses to spend more time on professional development overall. This was accounted for by two factors. Senior staff spent significantly (p<.001 linear trend) more time in meetings, especially on school premises and on weekdays, than teachers on lower statuses. Although the trend was linear, the threshold here was between staff on 'C' Incentive Allowances and above on the one hand, and those on 'B' allowances and below on the other. The 181 'C' allowance holders and above spent, on average, 3.2 hours per week in meetings, whereas the 165 'B' allowance holders and below spent 1.8 hours in meetings. At the extremes, National Standard Scale teachers spent 1.6 hours whilst deputy heads spent 5 hours a week. This strengthens the argument that most of the time in meetings might less sensibly be included in professional development than in administration since, if meetings on school premises were of a staff development nature, it might be expected that, generally speaking, all staff (or all staff in a department or faculty) would be involved in staff development meetings. Meetings concerned with management or administrative matters, however, would involve senior staff more, as was the case here. The second factor that affects senior staff time in professional development overall is that senior staff spent more time on reading professional journals, documents, etc., especially during weekdays (p<.05 linear trend). The threshold here was between 'B' and 'A' allowance holders.

Two other findings about time on aspects of professional development are of interest. First, teachers who spent more time in the week working alongside a colleague spent significantly (p<.01 linear trend) more time in meetings in school than those who spent less time working alongside colleagues. This is to be expected given that collaborative teaching tends to require collaborative planning and discussion, and often leads to informal discussion between those engaged in team teaching.

Second, teachers reporting that they were on fixed-term contracts spent significantly less time on all aspects of professional development, and particularly on course attendance, travel to courses and reading. The differences applied to all days, and weekdays, and were statistically significant (p<.01 analysis of variance). This suggests strongly that teachers on fixed-term contracts tended to be excluded from in-service provision more than other teachers, a position that would help marginalise them from the professional development programme of the school as a whole.

SUMMARY

The teachers spent eighteen hours per week on preparation and professional development combined, of which over ten hours were off school premises; thirteen hours were spent on preparation (including planning lessons, marking/recording and organising materials, etc.). Nearly ten hours were spent during the week and just over three at weekends. Over seven-and-a-half hours were spent on preparation off school premises. Teachers prepared more for teaching subjects in which they were qualified than for other subjects. The amount of time spent on preparation, however, was primarily influenced by the teachers' 'conscientiousness'. Professional development took up just over five hours a week, although using a stricter definition in-service training occupied two hours per week, some 4 per cent of the working week. Women spent more time on in-service training at weekends and younger and less experienced teachers spent less time in in-service training. Meetings occupied two-and-a-half hours a week, although senior staff spent significantly more time at them than others.

6

ADMINISTRATION AND OTHER ACTIVITIES

ADMINISTRATION

A large number of activities on which teachers spend their time are more concerned with the routines of the school as an organisation than with direct teaching and its associated preparation. For this reason we have used the term administration to cover all these activities. However, we recognise that the term itself can bear a range of meanings, and in its more normal usage tends to mean clerical and managerial activities, handling paperwork and engaging in meetings. In our use of the term such activities are included, but in addition a wide range of other activities is covered. The way we use administration, as a term covering several very disparate activities, is therefore unconventional. Twelve sub-categories of activity are involved. Of these twelve, only the first two, school administration and examination administration, would be considered conventionally as administration.

Time on administration overall

The overall picture for our two samples is given in Table 6.1. As in most other tables the total time is slightly less than the sum of the parts. This is because some overlap occurred if, for example, a teacher mounted a display during registration time. The significance of administration overall, as we defined it, in the working life of teachers is indicated by the amount of time spent on it, equivalent to eighteen hours a week. Three points should be made at this stage.

First, there was a substantially consistent picture across the

Table 6.1 Time spent on administration (hours per week)

Activity	Sample 1	Sample 2
School administration	5.7	5.3
Examination administration	1.7	0.8
Pastoral care	1.5	1.4
Parents	1.1	1.1
Displays	0.2	0.2
Supervision	0.8	0.9
Liaison	0.7	0.7
Assembly	0.6	0.6
Breaks (free)	2.4	3.4
Breaks (working)	2.3	1.5
Non-contact time	0.4	0.4
Registration	1.2	1.1
Breaks (free + working)	4.8	4.8
Supervision, registration, assembly	2.6	2.6
School and examination administration	7.3	6.2
All administration	18.1	16.8

two samples. The difference in total time on administration between the groups is almost entirely attributable to amounts of time on the first two sub-categories, that is, administration as conventionally understood. The explanation lies in the sample differences, with a greater proportion of senior staff in Sample 1. Senior staff spend more time than others on these two sub-categories.

Second, the main differences in proportions of time spent on sub-categories were in respect of examination administration and breaks. Sample 1 spent 9 per cent of all administration time on examination administration, whilst Sample 2 spent 5 per cent. This might reasonably be explained by the fact that Sample 2 data were collected in one week, in which relatively little administration time on examinations happened to be necessary. Sample 1 data, however, being collected across two terms, would be more likely to illustrate the extent of such demands, including administration of mock examinations for GCSE. The other difference is that Sample 1 spent proportionately less time in real breaks and more in working breaks than Sample 2, although this was in an overall framework where the two samples recorded almost identical amounts of time in the two kinds of break combined.

Third, nearly all the time recorded under these headings was spent on school premises. This is understandable in respect of such things as assembly and registration, but less obviously so in respect of school administration and examination administration, where paperwork might be taken home (see below, p. 111, for details of the extent to which these two activities were carried out at weekends, for example). It looks as though the work involved mostly has to be carried out at school, perhaps because of ease of access to records and files and the need to consult colleagues face to face, and perhaps because the teachers mainly involved in such work are given time free of teaching in the school day for administration and therefore carry it out in the time allocated then.

Two broad kinds of administration: in contact and out of contact with pupils

In the analysis used in this chapter, we have divided the time spent on the various sub-categories of administration overall into two broad groups. These are the activities when teachers are *in contact* with pupils and those when the teachers are *out of contact* with them. *In contact* comprises pastoral care, supervision, assembly and registration. *Out of contact* comprises school administration, examination administration, parents, displays, liaison, breaks (free and working) and non-contact time. There is some ambiguity here in respect of meetings with parents, since pupils may attend some parental discussions; of displays, since pupils sometimes are present when teachers are mounting displays; and of work in breaks, which may involve contact with pupils. In each of the three cases we had to make a judgement about the probable use of time. As regards meetings with parents, although it is true that pupils do participate in parental discussions on occasions, we took the view that the main contact was with parents and that it was not teacher–pupil contact in the same sense as, say, registration. In respect of displays, where these occurred during lessons, the time would already be counted as pupil contact by the analytical programme because teaching would have been recorded at the same time under teaching. In respect of work during breaks, there was a less clearcut judgement to be made, but we took the view that, since the industrial disputes of the mid-1980s, very little teaching of pupils would be carried out during breaks, although there might well be discussion with individual pupils. But we considered that most work in breaks would involve lesson planning, marking and meetings. These judgements need to be taken into account in our discussion of the proportions of time that teachers spend in contact and out of contact with pupils generally, in Chapter 3.

On the basis of the above distinction, the teachers spent 4.1 hours a week of administration in contact with pupils and 14.5 out of contact with them. The time spent in contact with pupils includes registering them, moving them around school, supervising them and attending assembly, as well as being involved in pastoral care, where the latter included disciplining individual pupils and attending to personal and welfare aspects of pupils' life in schools. This time is equivalent to about one quarter of the time that teachers spent teaching. Although this figure may be surprising to those outside schools, administration in contact with pupils is regarded as important, since these activities constitute the formal and informal opportunities for personal and social development of pupils. During this time teachers engage in conversations with pupils, listen to their problems and get to know them as individuals outside the sessions officially allocated to teaching.

Variations in time on administration

The general picture of administration given in Table 6.1 disguised some variation within Sample 1 according to the sex, age, experience and salary status of the teachers concerned. The difference according to sex is given in Table 6.2, which shows female teachers spending significantly ($p<.01$ analysis of variance) less time on administration overall than men.

Table 6.2 Time spent on administration, by sex

Sex	Sample 1 (hours per week)
Male	19.5
Female	16.9
All teachers	18.1

Table 6.3 Time spent on all
administration, by age

Age	Sample 1 (hours per week)
21–30	14.5
31–40	16.6
41–50	18.4
51+	20.0
All	18.0

Table 6.4 Time spent on all administration, by
salary status

Salary status	Sample 1 (hours per week)
National Standard Scale	15.1
Incentive Allowance 'A'	14.7
Incentive Allowance 'B'	15.8
Incentive Allowance 'C'	19.1
Incentive Allowance 'D'	18.7
Incentive Allowance 'E'	18.3
Deputy heads	31.3
All	18.1

Linear trend: $p < .0001$

There was also a significant ($p < .001$ linear trend) difference related to age, as is shown in Table 6.3.

Even more significant differences ($p < .001$ linear trend) emerged from the analysis of time on administration according to length of teaching experience and salary status. The data for salary status are given in Table 6.4.

These differences are largely explained by differences in time spent on school administration, where variations according to sex, age, teaching experience and salary status were most marked.

Women spent significantly ($p < .001$ analysis of variance) less time than men on school administration, some 4.7 hours as against 7.1 hours per week.

The relationship between age and school administration is shown in Table 6.5, with increasing amounts of time spent on school administration by older teachers. The difference was significant statistically ($p < .01$ linear trend).

Table 6.5 Time spent on school
administration, by age

Age	Sample 1 (hours per week)
21–30	3.1
31–40	5.2
41–50	5.9
51+	7.0
All	5.8

Table 6.6 Time spent on school administration,
by salary status

Salary status	Sample 1 (hours per week)
National Standard Scale	2.8
Incentive Allowance 'A'	3.0
Incentive Allowance 'B'	4.1
Incentive Allowance 'C'	5.6
Incentive Allowance 'D'	6.1
Incentive Allowance 'E'	6.6
Deputy heads	19.0
All	5.8

Linear trend: $p < .001$

However, the greatest level of statistical significance emerged in the relationship between time on school administration and length of teaching experience and position on salary status ($p < .001$ linear trend). Table 6.6 gives the data for salary status in respect of Sample 1.

It can be seen that, even if the distinctive position of deputy head is ignored, the trend through each successive salary status is clearcut, with each level spending progressively more time on school administration. Since salary level is itself associated with experience, age and sex to different degrees, the findings about school administration and these variables are themselves inter-related, although the dominant variable is salary status, as might be expected.

The picture about examination administration is less clearcut. There were differences in relation to the four variables similar to those associated with school administration but, in general, the differences were not statistically significant. The exception here was the existence of a weak relationship between age/ experience and time spent on examination administration, with older/more experienced teachers spending significantly ($p < .05$ linear trend) more time than younger teachers. This finding suggests that, although responsibility for the administration of school examinations is given to older and more experienced teachers, it was not seen as a responsibility solely for the most senior staff in terms of salary status.

We were able to combine time spent on school and examination administration and to examine its relationship to salary status. It was also possible to show the time spent overall and during weekdays only. The data are given in Table 6.7.

As might be expected, the pattern is as for school administration alone since that constitutes the largest single amount of time on any sub-category. The picture provided by this table is fairly close to being a mirror image, or at least an inverted image, of the data on time spent teaching, given in Chapter 4, Table 4.3. The difference is that whereas 'C' allowance holders did similar amounts of teaching to their junior colleagues, Table 6.7 shows that they did more school and examination administration than them. It helps explain why 'C' allowance holders spent longer hours overall on work than all other teachers except deputy heads, a point taken up below in the comment on Table 6.8 concerning supervision.

From Table 6.7 the extent to which the administration was carried out at weekends can be deduced. It can be seen that relatively little, only about an hour a week, was done at

Table 6.7 Time spent on school and examination administration, by salary status: overall and during weekdays

Salary status	Sample 1, hours per week	
	Overall	*Weekdays*
National Standard Scale	4.0	3.2
Incentive Allowance 'A'	4.1	3.5
Incentive Allowance 'B'	5.4	4.4
Incentive Allowance 'C'	7.7	6.4
Incentive Allowance 'D'	7.9	7.0
Incentive Allowance 'E'	8.8	7.2
Deputy heads	20.5	17.9
All	7.3	6.2

weekends, although deputy heads spent over two and a half hours at weekends on this kind of administration.

Pastoral care

There was a tendency for female teachers to spend significantly (p<.05 analysis of variance) more time than male teachers on pastoral care. The former spent 1.7 hours, the latter 1.2 hours per week on it. There was no association between age or experience and time on pastoral care. However, there was a tendency (p<.05 linear trend) for those on higher salary statuses, especially those holding 'C' and 'D' allowances, to spend more time than other teachers on pastoral care. We also found, somewhat to our relief, methodologically speaking, that teachers with a formal responsibility for pastoral care spent significantly (p<.001 analysis of variance) more time than other teachers on it. This suggests not only that our measures were valid but also, and more importantly from the point of view of pupil needs, that those holding such a responsibility took it seriously.

However, responsibility for pastoral care led to a more diffuse set of duties than the single category pastoral care. Teachers with this responsibility spent more time on a cluster of other activities, which can be thought of as loosely associated with the welfare aspects of school life. They spent more time than other teachers with parents and on supervision of pupils, although in both respects the differences were not statistically significant. They also spent significantly more time on liaison (p<.05) and in assembly (p<.001 analysis of variance) than other teachers. They had significantly (p<.05 analysis of variance) less time in breaks free of work than other teachers, possibly because they were engaged in pastoral care during breaks. Thus it looks as though those who held formal responsibility for pastoral care in the schools actually took on more welfare-associated tasks as a consequence. The teachers involved were more likely to be women, and on middle management salary positions, than very junior or very senior teachers.

Supervision

There was no statistical association between sex, age and length of teaching experience, and time spent on supervision. There

Table 6.8 Time spent on supervision, by salary
status: weekdays

Salary status	Sample 1 (hours per week)
National Standard Scale	0.7
Incentive Allowance 'A'	0.8
Incentive Allowance 'B'	0.6
Incentive Allowance 'C'	1.1
Incentive Allowance 'D'	0.8
Incentive Allowance 'E'	0.7
Deputy heads	1.6
All	0.8

was, however, a statistically significant (p<.01 linear trend) difference associated with salary status. Deputy heads and 'C' allowance holders spent more time than other teachers on supervision. The data are given in Table 6.8.

This table reflects, as do several others including the summary table 7.5 in Chapter 7, the fact that 'C' allowance holders' and deputy heads' patterning of work have some common features, including the fact that they worked longer hours overall than other teachers. This is a point we explore further in Chapter 7.

Liaison

There was no difference in time spent on liaison according to sex or length of experience of the teachers, but there was a strong association (p<.001 linear trend) between salary status and time spent on liaison. This was mainly due to the relatively large amounts of time spent by deputy heads and, to a lesser extent, 'C' allowance holders (again). The data are given on Table 6.9.

As regards other aspects of administration (i.e., displays, parents, breaks, assembly, non-contact time and registration/transition), there was no general pattern of associations with the sex, age, experience and salary status of the teachers. However, deputy heads spent significantly (p<.05 analysis of variance) less time (1.2 hours as against 2.4 hours a week) on breaks free of work; they had less (p<.05 analysis of variance) real non-contact time and carried out significantly (p<.001 analysis of variance) less registration/transition than other

Table 6.9 Time spent on liaison, by salary
status: weekdays

Salary status	Sample 1 (hours per week)
National Standard Scale	0.6
Incentive Allowance 'A'	0.4
Incentive Allowance 'B'	0.7
Incentive Allowance 'C'	0.9
Incentive Allowance 'D'	0.5
Incentive Allowance 'E'	0.6
Deputy heads	2.1
All	0.7

teachers. This latter activity was negatively associated with salary status in general ($p < .001$ linear trend), as might be expected.

Other variables

We were able to examine time spent on administration and other variables such as the size and type of school, responsibilities held by teachers and other variables on the questionnaire. In general there were few statistically significant associations. The main findings are listed below, grouped according to whether they are institutional or individual variables.

School size, type and age range catered for

There were few relationships with type of school, age range catered for or size of school. There was significantly ($p < .05$ analysis of variance) less supervision and assembly in 16+ institutions, as might be expected. There were significantly ($p < .01$ analysis of variance) shorter real (i.e., free of work) breaks in comprehensive, secondary modern and 'other' (i.e., mainly tertiary colleges) and longer real breaks in selective schools, grant-maintained and independent schools. Selective, independent and 'other' institutions spent significantly ($p < .05$ analysis of variance) less time in registration/transition than other schools. It is worth saying that the amount of time spent on all school administration was not associated with any particular size, type or age range of school.

Teacher characteristics

Teachers holding responsibility for a subject spent less time on school administration than other teachers, as did those teachers who taught at Key Stage 3 ($p<0.05$ analysis of variance). Teachers on temporary allowances had more real non-contact time than other teachers ($p<0.05$ analysis of variance).

OTHER ACTIVITIES

Teachers were asked to record three sub-categories under the main category of other activities. These were:

1 attendance at governors' meetings;
2 involvement in sports, clubs, orchestra, residential field trips, etc., outside timetabled teaching sessions; and
3 miscellaneous, a sub-category for any activity that the teachers could not code according to the coding system.

Table 6.10 provides data for the two samples.

It can be seen from Table 6.10 that the largest amounts of time, 2.4 hours and 1.7 hours a week, some 5 per cent of teachers' overall time, were spent on uncodable activities of a miscellaneous kind. This suggests that even our fairly complex coding system, despite its having been trialled with practising teachers, was not discriminating enough to identify some common activities. This is partly because the coding guidelines could not cover every eventuality without becoming so long that they would have discouraged participants. Some teachers wrote in describing the kind of activities that they had included in the miscellaneous sub-category. They included attendance at union meetings, writing the draft of a school/department policy statement and moving between sites on a split-site school.

Table 6.10 Time spent on other activities

Activity	Hours per week	
	Sample 1	Sample 2
Governors' meetings	0.2	0.0
Sports, clubs, etc.	1.5	1.1
Miscellaneous	2.4	1.7
All other activities	4.1	2.8

Table 6.11 Time spent on governors' meetings,
by salary status

Salary status	Sample 1 (hours per week)
National Standard Scale	0.0
Incentive Allowance 'A'	0.1
Incentive Allowance 'B'	0.1
Incentive Allowance 'C'	0.4
Incentive Allowance 'D'	0.2
Incentive Allowance 'E'	0.5
Deputy heads	2.6
All	0.2

There were very few statistical associations with the sex, age, experience and salary status of teachers. This was to be expected given the mixed-bag nature of the other activities. There was, however, a strong association ($p<.001$ linear trend) in Sample 1 between salary status and attendance at governors' meetings, as is shown in Table 6.11.

Senior staff, especially deputy heads and 'E' allowance holders, spent more time than other teachers in governors' meetings, although, once again, the profile of 'C' allowance holders is more like the senior staff than the others.

Other variables

We examined the variables on the questionnaire to see if there were any relationships between them and the time spent on other activities. In general, there were few, mostly relating to school type.

There were significantly ($p<.01$ analysis of variance) more other activities overall in the small number ($n=19$) of independent schools than in other schools, with the teachers in the former spending 7 hours a week on other activities, compared to the average for all schools of 4.1 hours. Part of the explanation for this is that teachers in independent schools spent significantly more time overall, and particularly at weekends, on sports, clubs, etc. In general, as well as teachers in independent schools those in grant-maintained, secondary modern and grammar schools spent more time on sports clubs, etc., than those in comprehensive schools ($p<.001$ analysis of variance). The finding about independent schools has to be set in the context of the overall amount of time that teachers in different types of school spent on work. Those in independent schools spent more time on work overall (62.7 hours a week compared to the average for all schools of 54.4). This was true for weekdays, and especially for weekends, with teachers in independent schools spending 9.8 hours on work at weekends compared to the average for all schools of 6.1 hours. It must be remembered that we were dealing with very small numbers of independent schools.

There were no other significant differences, except that teachers on temporary allowances spent significantly ($p < .05$ analysis of variance) more time on sports clubs, etc., than other teachers, as did younger teachers, although the latter difference was not statistically significant.

SUMMARY

Administration is a term used here to cover a wide range of routines, not connected with teaching, preparation and professional development. Taken together these activities occupy eighteen hours a week, a third of the teachers' working time. The teachers recorded over seven hours a week on administering aspects of the school or examination arrangements, and a further one-and-a-half hours on pastoral care. Time spent in registration/supervision/assembly took up just over two-and-a-half hours per week, and break times took up nearly five hours a week, about half of which time was taken up with work. Small amounts of time were taken up with parents' meetings, displays and liaison. Women spent more time on pastoral care and less time on school administration. Time on school administration was significantly related to high salary status. Teachers spent over four hours on other activities, including one-and-a-half hours a week on sports, clubs, orchestras and other extra-curricular activities, and a small amount of time attending governors' meetings. There were nearly two-and-a-half hours spent on miscellaneous activities that did not fit into the coding system.

7

TEACHERS AND MANAGERS

The previous chapters have provided a general picture of the work of the teachers in our samples. This picture was painted using the mean hours spent on work by all the teachers combined. However, the general picture disguised a pattern of workloads differentiated according to the salary position of the teachers and the responsibilities associated with the salary positions. In this chapter we present the data showing this differentiated patterning of work. The data are those relating to the 348 teachers in Sample 1 only, although we provide a comparative comment on Sample 2 where appropriate. This is because the thirty-six Sample 2 teachers were on contracts that gave them different salary allowances from, and ones that were not strictly comparable with, those in the mainland UK. In addition, there were small numbers of teachers in each salary position, and no deputy heads were involved.

SALARY STATUS

The salary status of teachers in the UK in 1990–1 was determined by the 1990 Pay and Conditions Third Report (Interim Advisory Committee 1990). This allowed for teachers to be placed on a National Standard Scale and, where appropriate, for them to be awarded one of five Incentive Allowances ('A', 'B', 'C', 'D' or 'E'). When we refer to salary status in this chapter we mean the above distinctions, and not the salary point within each allowance spine. Head teachers and deputy heads were paid according to a differently determined salary scale. Table 7.1 shows the numbers of teachers on each salary status in Sample 1.

One point needs to be made about Table 7.1 at this stage. By

Table 7.1 Salary status of teachers in Sample 1

Salary status	Number of teachers	%
National Standard Scale	51	15
Incentive Allowance 'A'	45	13
Incentive Allowance 'B'	69	20
Incentive Allowance 'C'	36	10
Incentive Allowance 'D'	99	28
Incentive Allowance 'E'	20	6
Deputy heads	26	8
Not recorded	2	<1
All	348	100

Table 7.2 Proportion of teachers on different salary statuses

Salary status	Sample 1 %	% nationally
National Standard Scale	15	40
Incentive Allowance 'A'	13	10
Incentive Allowance 'B'	20	26
Incentive Allowance 'C'	10	6
Incentive Allowance 'D'	28	15
Incentive Allowance 'E'	6	4
Deputy heads	8	n.a.

Source: Interim Advisory Committee (1990)

national comparisons, for example with the distributions in the 1990 Pay and Conditions Third Report, this is a skewed distribution. There are relatively few teachers on the National Standard Scale without allowances (15 per cent as against 40 per cent nationally). There are considerably more 'D' allowance holders (28 per cent as against 14.7 per cent). There are no head teachers in our sample. This skew means that conclusions about the overall patterning of teachers' work in the UK, especially the amounts of time spent on the different sub-categories, should be drawn with caution.

It is, however, possible to weight the different workload patterns of the teachers on different salary status, according to the expected national distribution. This is illustrated in Table 7.2.

Table 7.2 gives the distributions in Sample 1 and a national sample, derived from Table 12 of the Third Report (Interim Advisory Committee 1990). (Pages 30–1 of the Third Report point out the uncertain base for national comparison, but cite the LACSAB September 1989 survey which obtained a 70 per cent LEA response.) Table 12 of the Third Report does not include deputy heads, so direct comparison with the proportions in Sample 1 is not possible. However, if deputies are excluded from the calculation and the percentage on each scale is adjusted to match the IAC figures, the hours on work overall would be 53.7 hours per week. This is marginally reduced from the unweighted figure of 54.4 hours including deputy heads. Excluding deputies, the unweighted figure is 54.0 hours.

There are two conclusions. First, the skew in our sample has only a marginal effect on the total hours worked, since overall time spent on work was not significantly associated with salary status, except in the case of deputy heads. Second, the differential patterning of work, for example between teachers on different allowances, will not be affected by the skew since differential patterning refers to means *within* categories of teachers.

Table 7.3 Salary status of teachers in Sample 2

Salary status	Number of teachers	%
Basic Scale	7	19
Supplement 'A'	11	31
Supplement 'B'	15	42
Other	3	8
All	36	100

The salary status of teachers in Sample 2 is given in Table 7.3. These teachers were on either the basic scale or had one of three 'supplements' (similar to incentive allowances) for extra responsibilities. There were no deputy heads in this sample. The patterning of their work is shown in Table 7.4, mainly to allow comparison with Table 7.5, but the small numbers in Sample 2 must be remembered.

Table 7.4 Patterning of workloads, by salary status (Sample 2)

Activity	Mean hours per week				
	Basic Scale	Supplement 'A'	Supplement 'B'	Other	All
Teaching	18.6	19.1	17.0	18.9	18.1
Preparation	19.4	12.7	14.3	21.3	15.4
Administration	12.8	17.2	18.5	16.0	16.8
Professional development	2.3	1.7	3.4	2.8	2.6
Other activities	0.9	3.0	3.6	2.8	2.8
Total time	53.5	51.7	54.5	58.6	53.8

The patterning of workloads

Table 7.5 shows the patterning of workloads of the teachers in Sample 1 according to their salary status.

From Table 7.5 some points about the patterning of teachers' workloads become clear. First, deputy heads have a distinctively different profile of activities from all other teachers. Their work is characterised by the dominant 31.4 hours spent on administration, and by the very small amounts of time spent on teaching.

Second, the pattern most directly related to salary status concerns teaching. The higher the salary status the lower the amount of time that is spent teaching. The statistical trend here was highly significant (p<.001 linear trend).

There was a threshold or break point between Incentive Allowance 'C' and 'D'. For all practical purposes there was very little difference in the amounts of teaching carried out by the teachers on National Standard Scale, 'A', 'B' and 'C' allowance holders. Give or take a couple of minutes, they taught for three hours forty minutes per day. Teachers holding Incentive Allowances 'D' and 'E', and deputies, on the other hand, did significantly less teaching – three hours fifteen minutes, three hours and one hour forty-five minutes per day respectively.

Moreover, when we examined the ages of the pupils who were being taught by the teachers we also found a difference according to salary status. We found that the higher the teachers' status the less the teaching at Key Stage 3. The statistical significance here was high (p<.001 linear trend). At Key Stage 4 the same effect was observable although the statistical relationship, whilst significant, was weaker (p<.05 linear trend).

Table 7.5 Patterning of workloads, by salary status (Sample 1)

				Mean hours per week				
Activity	National Standard Scale	Incentive Allowance 'A'	Incentive Allowance 'B'	Incentive Allowance 'C'	Incentive Allowance 'D'	Incentive Allowance 'E'	Deputy heads	All
Teaching	18.4	18.3	17.9	18.2	16.3	15.0	8.8	16.9
Preparation	13.1	14.6	13.2	11.9	13.8	12.6	6.5	12.9
Administration	15.1	14.7	15.8	19.0	18.7	18.3	31.4	18.1
Professional development	3.7	4.0	4.9	5.5	5.8	6.9	9.5	5.3
Other activities	4.0	4.6	2.8	5.3	4.1	3.9	4.5	4.1
Total time	52.3	53.2	52.2	57.6	55.1	54.8	58.0	54.4

There was a relationship between salary status and sixth-form teaching, with teachers holding Incentive Allowances 'D' and 'E' (but not deputy heads) doing more sixth-form teaching in absolute terms than other teachers. Given that 'E' and 'D' allowance holders did less teaching anyway, the proportion of their teaching carried out with sixth forms was relatively very great. Of the teaching carried out by 'D' and 'E' allowance holders, 31 per cent was to sixth forms.

We were also able to examine the relationship of salary status and class size. Class size here refers to the classes 'as taught' in the terms of the DES statistics, rather than to teacher:pupil ratio in a school or to the size of registration groups. As might be expected, given the evidence outlined in the previous paragraph, there was a strong positive statistical relationship, with teachers higher up the salary status scale teaching smaller classes. The statistical significance was very high ($p<.001$ linear trend).

Third, it will be recalled that the broad category of administration included a range of activities such as meeting parents, registration, assembly, breaks, etc., which most teachers would engage in irrespective of salary status. The larger amounts of time on administration associated with Incentive Allowance holders 'C', 'D' and 'E' are accounted for by school/departmental administration, administration in connection with examinations or pastoral care/discipline. Deputy heads recorded 19 hours a week on school administration whilst, at the other extreme, teachers on National Standard Scale spent 2.7 hours on it.

The picture gained about preparation from Table 7.5 is slightly misleading at first glance. It looks as though preparation decreases as salary status rises. However, as indicated in Chapter 5, preparation needs to be considered in relation to the amount of teaching carried out. To do this it is sensible to use the ratio we presented in Chapter 5, whereby the amount of teaching is set against the amount of preparation. This is done in Table 7.6 below.

It can be seen that there are minor differences in the ratio of teaching to preparation, but they do not reveal a trend associated with salary status. 'C' allowance holders, National Standard Scale teachers, 'B' allowance holders and deputy heads have relatively low ratios, whilst 'A', 'D' and 'E' allowance holders have relatively high ratios. 'D' and 'E' allowance holders in particular do relatively little preparation in absolute terms, but spend proportionately more time on preparation for the amount of teaching that they do.

123

Table 7.6 Teaching:preparation ratio, by salary status

Salary status	Sample 1 teaching:preparation ratio
National Standard Scale	1:0.71
Incentive Allowance 'A'	1:0.79
Incentive Allowance 'B'	1:0.74
Incentive Allowance 'C'	1:0.65
Incentive Allowance 'D'	1:0.85
Incentive Allowance 'E'	1:0.84
Deputy heads	1:0.74
All	1:0.77

Professional development likewise appears at first glance to be patterned in a relationship suggesting that more professional development is engaged in by teachers in the higher salary statuses. In fact, as can be seen from the coding system (p. 12), our broad category of professional development included staff meetings (see the discussion of this point on p. 62). Nearly all the difference between teachers on different salary statuses is accounted for by the fact that senior staff engage in more meetings than junior staff. Once that element has been deducted there is no salary-related difference between teachers in respect of the time spent on professional development, except for deputy heads who spent more time on it. There is no trend in the time spent on other activities, a category which includes sports, orchestras, etc., attendance at governors' meetings and a miscellaneous sub-category. For example, whilst senior staff spent more time at governors' meetings, meetings were not frequent enough for this difference to have a statistically significant effect in the main overall category.

'C' allowance holders: the worst of both worlds?

The position of 'C' allowance holders stands out from the other teachers, except deputies. They work longer hours overall than all but the deputies, they do above average amounts of teaching and they spend more time on administration than all but the deputy heads. They spend more time than their juniors in professional development, and spend most time of all on other activities. Only in preparation do they spend less time than other teachers, both absolutely and in terms of the teaching:

preparation ratio; theirs is the lowest ratio of all teachers. This may be due to preparation being more 'compressible' than their other commitments. We do not know how typical this picture is but it suggests the need for further research.

Three pen portraits

We have decided to present further details on the patterning of work in Sample 1 by providing 'time distributions' for three groups of teachers, viz.: all teachers (n=348); deputy heads (n=21); and National Standard Scale teachers (n=51). These are provided in Figure 7.1 as a bar-chart.

Thus, we provide composite patternings of work for all the teachers in the study, and what might be regarded as the 'extremes' on either side of this average picture, namely those whose major responsibilities are managerial/administrative (the deputy heads) and those whose major responsibilities are instructional (National Standard Scale teachers).

All teachers

Figure 7.1 shows the work pattern for all 348 teachers, expressed as mean times spent on each activity. We can see that just under seventeen hours are spent on teaching (31 per cent of total time), fourteen of which are spent teaching the main subject. Of particular interest is the minute proportion of teaching time spent on National Curriculum assessment at Key Stage 3 (0.02 per cent of all time). All preparation takes up nearly thirteen hours a week, a ratio of preparation to teaching of 0.76:1. Of the 5.3 hours per week spent on professional development, almost half (2.6 hours) is spent in staff meetings and other meetings.

Administration takes up the longest amount of time, but it is a set of sub-categories which are not necessarily interrelated. Our composite secondary school teacher spends over seven hours a week on school and examination administration and one-and-a-half hours per week on pastoral care, often counselling or disciplining individual pupils. Breaks/lunchtimes occupy four-and-a-half hours a week, of which two-and-a-half hours are 'real' breaks, that is, free of work. Although the teachers nearly all had over three hours a week of non-contact time according to their questionnaire responses, only about twenty-four minutes

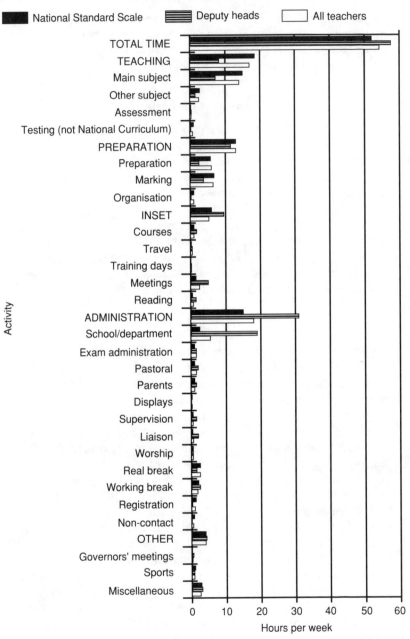

Figure 7.1 Distribution of categories of work, by salary status

of that time was actually recorded in the diaries as free of work. Registration and transition took up just over seventy minutes a week, about a quarter of an hour per day. Other activities comprised mainly time spent with orchestras, sports teams, school clubs, etc. (one-and-a-half hours per week), with two hours and twenty-four minutes on activities that the teacher could not fit into the coding system, e.g., moving between sites on a split-site school, filling in the record of time, time spent on union activities and other things.

Deputy heads

Figure 7.1 shows a very different patterning of work for deputy heads, who spent the longest hours on work overall (fifty-eight hours a week). A small proportion of this overall time, 15 per cent, was spent on teaching, equivalent to only one-and-three-quarter hours per day. Deputy heads spent six-and-a-half hours a week on preparation, giving a ratio of preparation to teaching of 0.7:1, only slightly less than the average. In other words, deputy heads do not appear to prepare less for the limited amount of teaching they do. Professional development accounts for 9.5 hours per week, five hours of which were spent in meetings of various kinds, including staff meetings. Deputies spent more time also on in-service courses, over two hours per week, and on reading documents (1.5 hours per week) than average.

Administration takes up nearly 31.5 hours per week, of which the longest time (nineteen hours) is given over to school administration. If we combine the four 'school management' codes – AA (school administration), AE (examination administration), AP (parents) and AL (liaison) – deputies were spending 24.3 hours per week on them. To this we could add the five hours on meetings. Thus, deputies were spending at least twenty-nine hours per week on administration, as conventionally understood. An important question which could not be examined in this study is how much of the twenty-nine hours was spent on activities needing deputies' high levels of managerial expertise/experience, and how much was on relatively low-level routine administrative or clerical tasks. It is likely that a substantial proportion of school administration and examination administration was low-level (see Torrington and Weightman 1989). This is an issue we explore further in Chapter 8.

National Standard Scale teachers

Figure 7.1 shows the pattern of teachers on the National Standard Scale. They work for slightly less time than the average. Teaching takes up 18.4 hours, equivalent to 35 per cent of their overall time. Preparation occupies just over 13 hours a week, a ratio of teaching to preparation of 1:0.71, slightly lower than average. In respect of professional development, these teachers spend less time in meetings and reading documents than other teachers.

Administration occupies only 15.2 hours per week, very few of which, some 2.7 hours, are spent on school administration. These teachers spend more non-contact time not working than average but, otherwise, other aspects of administration are as might be expected. Also as might be expected, these teachers' other activities are distinguished by their entire absence of participation in governors' meetings.

Contact with pupils

A final comparison is a simple analysis of the time spent with pupils, as against time spent away from them. For each of the three groupings of teachers the figures are as given in Table 7.7. Time spent with pupils is calculated by adding time in all teaching codes and AC (pastoral/discipline/counselling/guidance), AS (supervision at breaks/beginning/end of school day), AW (assembly/worship) and AR (registration/transition/collecting dinner monies, etc.).

These figures exclude time on sports, orchestra, etc. If these activities were included, the percentage of time in contact with pupils would be 41 per cent, for all teachers. Figures 7.2, 7.3 and 7.4 illustrate the differences for National Standard Scale teachers, deputy heads and all teachers by means of pie-charts.

Table 7.7 Time spent in contact with pupils

Salary status	Time spent with pupils	Time spent with pupils as a percentage of total time
National Standard Scale	22.4	43
Deputy heads	13.4	23
All	21.0	39

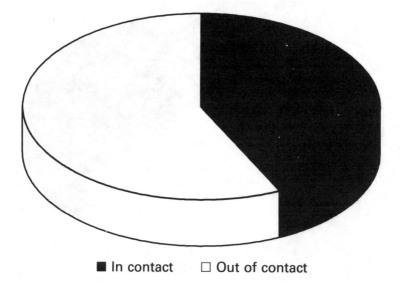

■ In contact   □ Out of contact

Figure 7.2   Contact and non-contact with pupils, National Standard Scale

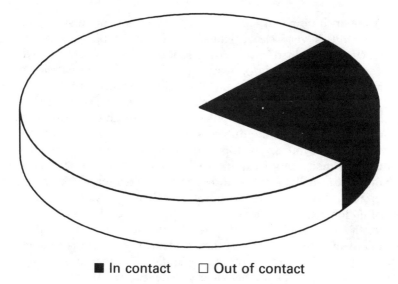

■ In contact   □ Out of contact

Figure 7.3   Contact and non-contact with pupils, deputy heads

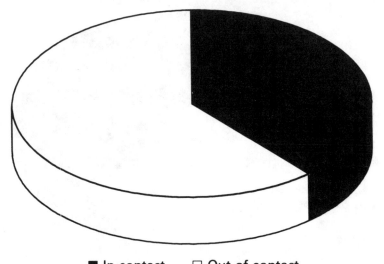

■ In contact □ Out of contact

Figure 7.4 Contact and non-contact with pupils, all teachers

MANAGERS AND TEACHERS

A major finding coming out of the statistics is not a surprising one, but is very clear. There is no such thing as a typical teacher's workload in secondary schools. There are at least two, very different, kinds of workload, defined by the balance of activities across work overall. We call these workload types the 'Managers' and the 'Teachers'. At the risk of creating false caricatures by reifying the poles of the factor given in Table 7.8, we can summarise the differences as follows.

'Managers' are on the top three salary status levels, are older, usually male, more experienced, do relatively less teaching, mostly to smaller groups, and spend much of their working time in administration and meetings. 'Teachers' are younger, more often female, less experienced, on the lower of the salary status levels, and some are on fixed-term contracts. They spend relatively large amounts of time on teaching, which is to larger groups, and engage in more preparation and marking.

The two groups are *not* clearly distinguished by the amount of time overall that they spend on work (although deputy heads work the longest hours of all teachers), but by the *balance* of their activities within the overall time. This differentiation by balance of workload may reflect a split in the organisation and culture of the school as a workplace. Some teachers, promoted to Incentive Allowance 'D' and above, carry out much of their work as managers or administrators for the school, whilst others carry proportionately more of the teaching in the school, especially if account is taken of teaching productivity as we have defined it in Chapter 4. We can demonstrate the existence of such a split in two ways. Figures 7.5 and 7.6 illustrate through bar-charts salary status in relation to amount of teaching and of school administration respectively. Second, the 'Managers' factor in the factor analysis given in Table 7.8 demonstrates the dominant effect of status.

The multiple regression analysis showed that salary status was the factor most clearly predicting the amount of time that a teacher spent on all administration. The association was highly significant statistically ($p<.001$). There was even greater

Table 7.8 Factor analysis: Factor 1: the 'Managers' factor

Questionnaire variable	Loadings on Factor 1
Experience	0.81346
Age	0.66393
Salary status	0.63879
Non-contact time	0.28770
Fixed-term contract	0.27126
Re-training	0.12243
Time spent teaching main subjects	−0.10674
Typicality of time spent in other terms	−0.14973
Responsibility for other aspects	−0.24634
Temporary allowance	−0.33475
Female	−0.34515
Time spent teaching alongside colleagues	−0.40806

Note: This 'Managers' factor represents the most clearcut grouping of the questionnaire responses; it is dominated by the 'managerial' criteria of experience, age and salary status. Salary status was selected as representative of these three for the multiple regression analysis, as the most likely to affect work duties. The less strongly loaded items (e.g., 'female') also appeared on other factors of the analysis, which represented aspects of working practice such as time spent on collaborative teaching. They were therefore included as separate items in the multiple regression analysis.

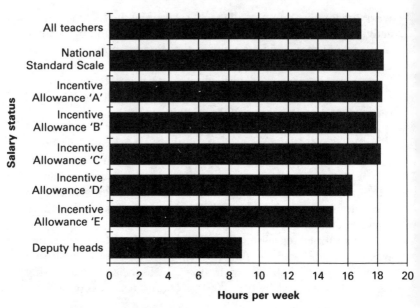

Figure 7.5 Time spent on teaching, by salary status

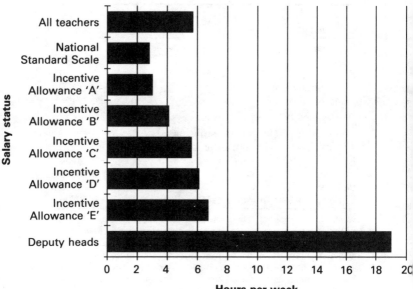

Figure 7.6 Time spent on school administration, by salary status

132

significance (p<.001) when the code AA alone (school admini-stration) was examined in relation to salary status. Conversely, the multiple regression analysis showed that the amount of time spent teaching was most strongly predicted by the salary status of the teacher – the lower the status the more teaching (p<.001). In addition, the best predictor of time spent in meetings on school premises was salary status (p<.001), with senior staff spending more time.

SUMMARY

We can summarise the findings as follows.

First, there is a strong (p<.001) positive linear trend relating higher positions on the salary scale to long hours on school and examination administration. Our data do not allow us to distin-guish clearly between managerial and administrative activities. 'D' and 'E' allowance holders and deputy heads average 1.8 hours per day on administration, whilst National Standard Scale and 'A' and 'B' allowance holders average forty-six minutes per day. At the extremes, deputy heads spend 20.6 hours per week on such administration, whilst National Standard Scale teachers spend four hours per week.

Second, there is a strong (p<.001) negative linear trend relating salary scale and time spent teaching. 'D' and 'E' allowance holders and deputy heads spend 13.8 hours a week teaching, whilst National Standard Scale and 'A', 'B' and 'C' allowance holders spend over eighteen hours per week. Deputy heads (8.75 hours per week) spend less than half as much time on teaching as National Standard Scale teachers (18.4 hours). We take up the management issues related to this split in Chapter 8.

Part II

TEACHER PROFESSIONALISM AND CHANGE

8

THE USE OF TEACHERS' TIME

Some management issues

THE WORK OF TEACHERS: A COMPARATIVE PERSPECTIVE

A recent report (International Labour Office 1991) on the work of teachers in both developing and industrialised societies argued that teachers' work was determined largely as a function of two variables: hours of work in and out of school, and class size. A previous report (International Labour Office 1981) had pointed out the tendency of governments to underestimate teachers' workload and the intensity of teaching.

The 1991 report rehearsed the changing nature of teaching as new demands were placed upon the schools. These included designing and implementing curriculum reforms, introducing new forms of assessment and engaging in in-service training for up-dating of skills. More broadly, teachers were being expected to impart understanding of, and positive attitudes towards, the world of work and other countries. New technology and new teaching methods were also required, and special programmes for multi-culturalism, integration of children of migrant workers and mainstreaming children with special educational needs were tasks facing most contemporary teachers. There was an accelerating trend for moral and social responsibilities previously exercised by parents, churches and local communities to be transferred to schools, with consequent changes in the teachers' role.

Summarising the impact of these changes on teachers' work in over forty countries, the report noted:

The main trends in hours worked over the past decade are defined by a number of common features. First, though

137

the number of actual teaching hours in contact with students has remained static, or even decreased slightly in most countries . . . the overall workload of teachers appears to have increased. The main growth areas of work are administrative duties to conform to additional rules and regulations, and the attention devoted to unruly pupils. Secondly, work in the evenings and on weekends remains a steady, though irregular, component of teachers' working time . . . . Thirdly, stress and time pressures increasingly characterise the working day of most teachers.

(International Labour Office 1991, pp. 84–6)

Moreover, preparation time had increased under educational reforms; administrative and clerical tasks (e.g., meetings with parents, in-service training, correspondence, curriculum development meetings) were taking up an increasing proportion of teachers' work; and supervision and disciplinary tasks had taken on increased significance.

There are some methodological weaknesses in the ILO report, especially because it relied principally upon official statements about teachers' hours and conditions. However, the general picture of the changing demands upon teachers is supported by an overview of national policies on teacher professionalism (OECD 1990). Summarising the 'new challenges' facing teachers in twenty-one OECD countries, the OECD report noted:

The political pressure to quicken the pace of educational reform had inevitable consequences for the demands made on teachers . . . [who] are increasingly voicing concern about the sheer availability of time and about their preparedness as a body to do justice to these different challenges. It is in the interests of all that the extension of the teachers' role should constitute a source of professionalism based on expertise rather than be simply burdensome additions of ever greater numbers of new responsibilities . . . . From the stand-point of the classroom teacher and school principal, what matters is that they are expected to promote these strategies actively, and all at once . . . . Changes that are at present introduced discretely and piecemeal may call for the comprehensive review of institutional structures and classroom organisation, taking

account of teachers' duties – individually and collectively
– in their entirety.

(OECD 1990, pp. 113–14)

These international studies therefore illustrate the twofold pressures upon teachers arising from trends in the larger
society: a diffusing of the role expectations so as to reduce the
proportion of working time spent teaching, and intensification
of demands arising from bolt-on approaches to educational
policy-making.

SECONDARY TEACHING IN THE UNITED KINGDOM

The general argument of this chapter is twofold. First, our
evidence about secondary teachers in the UK in 1990–1 is in line
with the international trends outlined above in respect of hours
of work and the diffuse nature of teacher responsibilities.
Second, some fundamental questions for the management of
secondary schools arise from the nature of educational policy
here, as the last sentence in the OECD extract quoted above
implies about the cross-cultural evidence. In the UK, a series of
'reforms', concentrating upon assessment, the curriculum and
school management, have hit the schools in an unco-ordinated,
and even unconnected, sequence, with existing demands on
teachers not being allowed for. Duffy (1993), a former president
of the Secondary Heads' Association, explained the opposition
to National Curriculum testing in secondary schools in 1993 by
illustrating from his own school the lack of recognition of the
overall demands on teachers. In this situation the schools'
priorities tended to take precedence over those of the government,
especially where incompatible policies operated:

I've looked at the obsessive detail of the marking schemes
[for National Curriculum assessment] and at the endless
pages of instruction about aggregation and recording and
I've come to suspect that the whole exercise was almost
literally impossible. How on earth, I wonder, could we
have *done* all this, as well as all the other things that we
had to do in June? This week, at our monthly planning
meeting (don't laugh; some schools remain absurdly opti-
mistic) I looked around the table and saw the answer on

my friends' and colleagues' faces. There is no doubt about it, the pressure shows.

So what, if we had done those tests, would we have sacrificed? Mentally, I count off on my fingers the June commitments that came on top of teaching. Assessments and examination for Years 10 and 12, of course – and after those, by sensible tradition, the field course weeks. In-house assessments, as always, for Year 9; reports to parents for all three years, as good practice and now in ever greater detail the law decrees. (Does anybody up there begin to realise, incidentally, what confusion they have caused by that off-the-cuff decision to change the language of assessment in Year 10? We were just begin-ning to get our students and their parents used to the relativities of the ten-point attainment scale. Out of the blue we learn that GCSE is to retain this year its incom-patible letter scale. So how do we grade the course work, and chart progress on reports? That's a question that isn't answered on any marking scheme.)

But back to my list. What about our post-sixteen induction course – or our two industrial input team-building days? Or two concerts? Or the training weekends for the Duke of Edinburgh award? Or the Hello and Welcome evenings for next year's Year 9 intake and their parents? Or the student/teacher/parent/governor working party on bully-ing? Or the 'Any Questions' evening for the parents and friends . . . . Or the work we did on our in-school values statement?

I'm not pretending for a moment that any of this is particularly special. It's the sort of commitment that has been at the heart of every worthwhile school that I have ever known. But I do think that it is being put at risk by the avalanche of contradictory orders and instructions that rumbles down incessantly from distant heights and adds immeasurably to the teacher's workload.

(Duffy 1993, p. 48)

EVIDENCE ABOUT THE CHANGING NATURE OF TEACHERS' WORK

It is not our intention comprehensively to review the literature on the management of secondary schools, which has been done elsewhere (e.g., Fletcher-Campbell 1988, Earley and Fletcher-Campbell 1990, Weightman 1988). For our purposes we would draw attention to three aspects of teachers' work particularly germane to our research.

First, as we have shown in Chapter 1, the extensiveness of secondary teachers' work, i.e., the hours typically worked by teachers, was first mapped out by Hilsum and Strong's (1978) study, based on 201 teachers in 72 schools in Surrey in 1974. They arrived at a figure of 46.75 hours per week. More recently, three surveys (NAS/UWT 1990, 1991, Lowe 1991), with differing methodologies, provided evidence that secondary teachers were typically working between fifty and fifty-five hours per week in term-time. Taken with our findings, they constituted a prima facie case that workloads in the UK had increased substantially since Hilsum and Strong's study, although unlike the latter they were not based on direct observational techniques.

Second, a focus on the work of middle management had characterised much of the analysis, following Marland's (1971) pioneering book. The reasons include, according to Earley and Fletcher-Campbell (1990), the fact that about a third of teachers have formal managerial responsibilities, defined as 'responsibility for achieving the school's goals by working through, and with, other professional teachers, which [is] separate and different from their classroom management roles' (McMahon and Bolam 1987, p. 3). Heads of departments and faculties have been seen as crucial to the effective operation of secondary schools (Weindling and Earley 1987), although Earley and Fletcher-Campbell (1990) point out the need to distinguish between *managerial* skills on one hand and *organisational/administrative* skills on the other. This is an issue we explore later in this chapter. An interesting development, spearheaded by Knight (1989, 1991) has examined alternative management of time in the school day.

A disadvantage of the focus in the literature on middle management is that it appears to have neglected the role of relatively junior teachers, despite the fact that the Teachers' Pay and Conditions Act identified the 'co-ordination of the work of other teachers' as one of the responsibilities of teachers on the National Standard (then, Main) Scale.

Third, teacher professionalism, teacher careers and teacher supply/shortages have been a continuing concern in the literature on the politics of teaching. There has been international interest in the politics of teachers' work (e.g., Connell 1985, Lawn and Grace 1987, Reyes 1990) and in teacher professionalism and teacher organisations (Hoyle 1980, Ozga and Lawn 1981, Lawn 1985, Ozga 1988, Poppleton and Riseborough 1990). A common thesis here is the 'de-professionalisation', 'de-skilling' or 'proletarianisation' of teachers, as union influence has been eroded and central control increased. We examine this further in Chapter 9. A perspective on teachers' careers (Sikes *et al.* 1985), and in particular gender-related opportunities (e.g., Purvis 1981, De Lyon and Widdowson-Migniuolo 1989, Skelton 1987, Evetts 1990), has also characterised recent work, in which it is argued that female teachers are disadvantaged in career opportunities.

Insofar as all these studies have placed teaching as work into a central frame of analysis they are useful, but they have three substantive limitations.

First, there has been no attempt to build upon, extend or test the empirical baseline data established by Hilsum and his colleagues in the early and mid-1970s. This concerned mundane, but for the teachers highly significant, parameters of work, such as the amount of time spent, the balance of time across different components, both on and off school premises, and factors in their working conditions affecting both the realisation of teaching goals and teachers' personal lives. In particular, the concentration on gender-differentiated opportunities in educational careers may have helped to distract attention from factors in the workplace of *all* teachers, irrespective of status or gender.

Second, teacher commitment has been almost entirely neglected, with the notable exceptions of Fullan and Hargreaves's (1991) questioning of the excessive identification of Canadian teachers with their work, and the NFER study (Earley and Baker 1989) of teacher retention.

Third, the statutory intrusions upon teachers' work of the

Teachers' Pay and Conditions Act 1987 and the Education Reform Act 1988 have been so pervasive, recent and immediate as to bring into question the relevance of most analyses that pre-date them. In particular, the local management of schools has brought into more local focus employee–employer relations, not least through the responsibility given to governing bodies for appointment and dismissal of teachers and budget management, teacher appraisal and performance-related pay. The detailed impact of such changes on the experience of teaching as work, workplace relations of teachers and their working conditions cannot be examined by means of macro-analyses of teacher careers and teacher–state relationships focused on the extra-school context.

However, an emerging group of studies relates to the work of teaching under the Education Reform Act. Two studies (Busher and Saran 1990, Maclure and Marr 1990) of teaching as work in the post-1987 context identified a widening definition of teaching, apparently confirming the ILO and OECD conclusions quoted earlier. Busher and Saran, for example, argued that teachers were seen as responsible for a wide range of activities in addition to teaching, including administration, in-service training and management. In this, they are echoing not merely the ILO and OECD reports but the comments of Hilsum and Strong, quoted in Chapter 1, pages 4–5.

They identified three problems which they traced to the post-1987 context: the use of teachers' time; alienation from, or reduced identification with, teaching as an occupation or a career; and widespread disaffection arising from the workloads created by obligations under the 1988 Act. All three, if confirmed in other work, will have significant implications for the management of schools. Our findings refer directly to the first of these in particular, as well as casting light on the workload dimension. They have implications for school management which are explored below.

MANAGEMENT ISSUES

We are not in a position to examine the management of secondary schools in a general or comprehensive way. However, three issues arise from our findings. They are: the use of teachers' time; match of expertise to teaching; and gender and teachers' work.

However, we preface our discussion by reiterating the points made by the OECD report and by Duffy's illustration, both quoted earlier in this chapter. Management of individual schools has had to operate in a policy context of considerable turbulence, which makes rational planning difficult; because of the lack of a coherent policy on curriculum and assessment (especially at Key Stage 4 where examination modes and reporting and recording systems considered successful have been found to be incompatible with National Curriculum requirements); and because the pace of change required is seen as unrealistic. The fact that this syndrome is a cross-national characteristic of change is unlikely to be of comfort to those involved in implementing change in the schools.

THE USE OF TEACHERS' TIME

We have shown in Chapter 7 that there were two broad categories of teachers, distinguished by the different structuring of their time. The 'Managers' spent large amounts of time on school administration and relatively little time teaching, whereas the 'Teachers' spent little time on school administration and relatively large amounts of time on teaching. It is possible to exaggerate this distinction, but the statistical analysis indicates very highly significant differences between the use of time of teachers on National Standard Scale and Incentive Allowances 'A', 'B' and 'C' on the one hand, and those on Incentive Allowances 'D', 'E' and deputy heads on the other.

Our data do not allow us to distinguish the extent to which the activities coded as school administration were *managerial* (i.e., involving high-level skills) or *administrative* or *clerical* (requiring low-level skills). However, other research, e.g., Torrington and Weightman's study (1989), *The Reality of School Management*, suggests it is probable that substantial amounts of time per week were being spent by the highest-paid teachers on relatively low-level routine tasks, often of a clerical nature. They quote, tendentiously (p. 101), a deputy head who said, 'What this school needs is fewer deputies and more clerks. Any literate sixteen-year-old could do this.' They distinguish between *technical* work (e.g., marking, teaching, anything directly involving pupils), *administrative* work ('organisational maintenance' such as filling in forms and lists, arranging furniture, telephoning, photocopying, etc.) and *managerial* work (which involves setting precedents, influencing others to assent to decisions, ensuring that agreed policies are put into practice, etc.). Pointing out that all staff spend time on all three categories, Torrington and Weightman provide evidence of seventy teachers, observed for a day or half a day. They were from senior and middle management (i.e., heads, deputies, year heads, department heads, subject heads or others). One conclusion they draw is particularly germane to our evidence. They say (p. 102):

> Perhaps the most stunning figure is the average amount of time Deputies (31 per cent), Senior Teachers (27 per cent), Heads of Pastoral (29 per cent) and curriculum areas (24 per cent) spend on low-grade clerical duties, that is administrative work.

They explain the attraction of such work to senior staff as the relative ease there is in getting it completed, and the conflation of administrative and managerial tasks in teachers' minds. They nonetheless draw the conclusion (p. 103) that, 'It is ridiculous to see well-paid professionals doing work that a properly trained administrator or clerk could do better.'

It is not clear to us how Torrington and Weightman established the representativeness of the days or half days observed in these cases, and their proportions of time refer to the *observed school day* (i.e., excluding work away from school) so that the proportions might need to be adjusted in the light of the actual balance of activities across a whole day or week or term. Nonetheless, the proportions they identify are not incompatible with our figures even though, for the above reasons, they do not enable direct comparison. For example, they showed (p. 102) deputies spending 71.5 per cent of the observed day on administrative and managerial tasks combined, and 21 per cent on technical tasks, mostly teaching and marking, presumably. Our deputies spent (see Chapter 7, p. 127), at the minimum, 50 per cent of their working week on administrative and managerial tasks and 26 per cent on teaching and preparation (including marking).

Torrington and Weightman's discussion of this feature of the work of senior staff in secondary schools is tinged with disapproval. They quote their project secretary, who had been typing up segments of the observation records of the deputies, as saying, 'Is that what they do? I could do that!' However, the responsibility for this situation is less the deliberate decision-making of schools and much more a consequence of institutional inertia combined with the unpredictable policy climate in which the schools have had to operate in the 1980s and early 1990s. This had encouraged, as Duffy (1993) argued in the quotation above, a tendency for schools to continue innovating but along their own priorities, and made long-term rational planning of the best use of staff time more difficult. Under the local management of schools, however, as Torrington and Weightman suggest, questions about the use of time of relatively well-paid professionals are bound to be asked, and management, faced with the kind of evidence about their own schools that we found about the teachers in our study, will have to move towards answers.

Responsibility for this situation is not attributable to the teachers themselves but is a policy issue for school management as a whole, especially for the head teacher and the governing body. It is worth their examining the current use of senior teachers' time to see if the provision of more support staff (to whom delegation of routine administration could be made) would enable both their managerial and their teaching skills to be exploited more effectively than is the case for many at present.

An alternative view is that the occupational split between 'Teachers' and 'Managers' is inevitable, given the managerial complexity of contemporary secondary schools and the increasing delegation of managerial responsibility to individual schools. On this view, the time of a few highly paid staff should be used almost entirely for management, policy-making and implementation, supported by more administrative and clerical staff. The patterning of the time of the rest of the staff should be more like that of the 'Teachers' in this study, with relatively large amounts of time spent on teaching. On this pattern the status structure in schools would become less pyramidical and flatter. This would formalise the split we have identified in the occupational culture of the schools, although it is likely to lead to more oppositional attitudes within schools between the 'Teachers' and the 'Managers'. It would move teachers' professional development, and the management of schools, towards the systems in some states in the USA, where clearcut careers in educational

administration are seen as alternative, rather than comple-
mentary, to teaching. For such a development to be worth the
potential risk to relationships in schools, it would be essential
for senior staff to be freed from routine administrative activities
so that their time could be used to good effect in management,
strategic planning and policy-making. They might also have to
spend more time than they do currently on the maintenance of
good relationships with the 'Teachers'. This view might be
developed, especially in schools where a rather straightforward
and uncomplicated perception is taken of value for money. In
such a perception, the most highly paid staff ought not to be
used for teaching since to do so will cost the school twice as
much as is needed to get the teaching done by a teacher on the
National Standard Scale.

However, the issue is not merely a matter for the local management of schools. There are national implications concerning the
use of Incentive Allowances, the development of pay flexibilities
and performance-related pay. It is technically possible, under
the Teachers' Pay and Conditions Document (Interim Advisory
Committee 1990), to award incentive allowances (especially the
'A' allowance) for 'outstanding abilities as a classroom teacher'.
Currently, as our data show, *reduction* in teaching load may be
construed as the main reward, consequence or spin-off of
progression through the pay structure. This view is deeply
embedded in the occupational culture and would make any
dramatic change, such as the award of the larger Incentive
Allowances for continuing to teach a full load, difficult to
implement. It is possible to see this culture as working in the
interest of male teachers, since a change in the direction at
which we are hinting above would benefit female teachers more.

There are two further difficulties. First, according to evidence
submitted to the School Teachers' Review Body (Interim Advisory
Committee 1990), the distribution of Incentive Allowances and
discretionary pay depends more on contextual factors such as
school size (and therefore their *availability*) than on the operation
of rational principles according to the pre-specified criteria of
the School Teachers' Pay and Conditions Document. Second,
the 'performance' by which performance-related pay might be
awarded would differ depending on the status of the teachers.
There would be difficulty in using a common set of perfor-
mances by which, say, the 'Teachers' and the 'Managers' in our

terms might be judged fairly in a competition for limited further allowances. It may be argued, understandably, that the schools are in a period of transition with regard to management. However, the pressures from the occupational culture outlined above, the problems of common performance indicators, a career progression favouring males and the financial disincentives against awarding the highest allowances for good teaching alone all point in the same direction. Excellent performance in the classroom is likely to continue to be rewarded by progressive removal from it.

MATCH OF SUBJECT EXPERTISE TO TEACHING DUTIES

We have shown (see Chapter 4, pp. 81–4) that generally the teachers were well matched to their teaching duties, if the main subject(s) of the teachers' initial training were taken as the basis for the analysis. We called this *objective* match. However, we showed that *subjectively*, viz., whether the teachers considered that their academic background was well matched to current teaching, the match was less good. We showed variations by subject in this respect, with technology being particularly poorly matched.

The match of teacher knowledge to teaching duties is a central concern of school management and has been seen as critical to the quality of the teaching and learning in secondary schools. The White Paper, *Better Schools* (1985), raised the issue in a sharp way: 'Good teaching depends heavily on a reasonable match between the qualifications and experience of teachers and the subjects they teach' (para. 26).

Smithers and Robinson (1991) found one in eight classes (Years 7–9) and one in ten classes (Years 10–11) taught by teachers lacking training in the subject taught. Both figures are not out of line with our findings in Table 4.1 (Chapter 4) that 15 per cent of time was spent on other subject(s), not on the teacher's main subject.

However, Merson (1989), in a detailed analysis of the concept and its use in official statements, showed that if you took match as being the relationship between two sides of the equation – the academic background and the teaching duties on which staff are deployed – there were varying levels: in teacher qualification there was the subject component, professional aspects and age range focus of the training. He cites the Secondary Staffing Survey, details of which were published in the Statistical Bulletins 8/86 (Department of Education and Science 1986) and 10/87 (Department of Education and Science 1987), to the effect that, on average, secondary school staff had qualifications in 2.5 subjects, held at different levels from a subsidiary subject in a Certificate of Education to the subject in a single honours degree course.

Merson also notes that the degree of match varies and comments that the *Cockcroft Report* (Department of Education and Science 1982) attempted to establish a simple hierarchy, from 'good', through 'acceptable' to 'nil'. He also notes that the date of initial qualification comes into play, especially where recent substantial changes to the conception of the subject have been developed. He shows that this has happened particularly in what is now called technology, but was formerly craft, and that such radical alterations to the concept of a subject since initial qualification are 'straining match with initial qualifications' (Merson 1989, p. 172). He notes that RE, conceived twenty years previously as a rather prescriptive subject focused on Christian scripture, is shifting towards contemporary study of a multi-faith nature.

The other side of the equation in Merson's view is 'even more complicated' – the year group to which the subject is taught, the ability grouping of the pupils, the felt need of school management to provide some subjects, such as personal and social education, that are not well matched to anyone's initial qualification, and the increasing need to provide cover teaching for absent staff.

Merson's paper argues for better evidence about match, and especially evidence about the relationship between match and the quality of teaching and learning. He also acknowledges that the ambiguity he detects in official statements and the conflicting evidence about the degree of match may service a national policy on teacher supply in which 'teacher shortages' can be defined flexibly.

Despite the conceptual problems, match remains a key issue when staff are being appointed to a school and when they are being allocated their teaching duties. Our evidence suggests four conclusions for the management of schools. First, small schools, as might be expected, have to operate with a greater degree of mis-match than larger schools, and teachers in them have to teach more subjects in which they are unqualified. Second, teachers' subjective perceptions of match enter into the equation in a way that reveals greater mis-match than would be the case if schools simply took initial qualifications into account. This varied by subject, by date of the teacher's initial training and by curriculum change, as Merson argued. Third, in respect of the link between match and quality, we provide statistically strong evidence that when teachers teach subjects for which they are not well qualified they spend less, not more, time on preparation. Although part of the explanation may lie in 'covering' for teachers who have left work for their classes to do whilst they themselves are absent, another part may lie in the tendency of secondary teachers to prepare and mark more thoroughly and more extensively the subject to which they have a professional commitment and with which they identify. Our evidence is, at the very least, suggestive of the idea that poor match will lead to less good teaching insofar as the latter depends upon time spent planning for and marking the pupils' learning.

Our evidence about objective match is, of course, rather limited since it assumes a direct connection between the degree subject studied at university and the syllabus and methods involved in the school curriculum. For example, two teachers with identical degrees in English literature might be faced with very different syllabuses in their school setting. If one is in a sixth-form college teaching 'A' Level English literature courses it would be reasonable to talk of her background as being well matched to her teaching duties. Another may be teaching remedial English to groups of pupils with special educational needs, English in business studies courses and courses in which there is emphasis on information technology, language awareness, grammar, syntax and punctuation. Her university course in English Literature may or may not have prepared her well for such teaching, but it is unlikely that it is sensible to regard her background as matched equally well to her teaching duties as that of the first teacher.

Objective match in particular is not a reliable guide where changes have been introduced into the school curriculum which challenge or cut across the categories of university subjects. The most obvious example is the introduction of broadly based integrated science courses, for which a graduate in a single science subject (say biology) will not necessarily be well matched, since the new science courses require the teaching of physics and chemistry as well as biology.

A final management issue here relates to the forecasting of teacher competence and the identification of in-service training needs. Which of the measures of match is used determines how great the problem is perceived to be. Using the objective measure, as the DFE does, has the administrative advantage of definition by clear criteria and the political advantage of showing the shortage at the lower limit, whilst disguising the teachers' view of the adequacy of their academic backgrounds. But the subjective measure may be much more real to the teachers involved and to the school management. This should therefore be the measure used by management in identifying training needs.

GENDER AND SECONDARY TEACHERS' WORK

The first finding to emphasise is that there was no significant difference in the amount of time on work overall by men and women teachers, on school premises or off, during weekdays or at weekends. Within overall time and salary categories there was no difference between men and women in the time spent on preparation or teaching, or professional development.

However, there were three principal gender differences in the patterning of work.

First, women spent significantly less time than men on administration overall ($p<.01$), and especially on school administration ($p<.001$), but they spent more time on pastoral care ($p<.05$).

Second, women taught Key Stage 3 pupils more ($p<.01$) and sixth-formers less ($p<.05$) than men did.

Third, although there was no difference in time overall on professional development, we found that women spent more ($p<.05$) time on in-service courses at weekends. This may be partly explained by the ability of women to meet in-service commitments more easily at weekends than in 'twilight' hours or in weekdays after school. This explanation is supported by the fact that women recorded more travel to in-service courses at weekends.

151

Table 8.1 Salary status, by sex

Salary status	Male	Female
National Standard Scale	14	36
Incentive Allowance 'A'	9	32
Incentive Allowance 'B'	25	42
Incentive Allowance 'C'	17	19
Incentive Allowance 'D'	61	37
Incentive Allowance 'E'	11	8
Deputy heads	13	12
Total	150	186
% of total	44.6	55.4

Chi square 29.8
d.f.6
p<.001

Our conclusions here are complex since the interaction of gender and workplace is not straightforward.

First, women do not 'put in less time' than men. There was no evidence to support the idea that these women, for reasons to do with demands on their time in the domestic setting, were able to commit themselves less to work than men. Second, and related to the first point, women teachers were paid less than men because fewer were on the higher Incentive Allowances. The differences in salary status were highly significant statistically, as Table 8.1 shows.

If the sexes were distributed randomly amongst the salary scales we would expect the numbers at each level to approximate to the 45/55 sex balance in the sample as a whole and to be roughly similar, with perhaps one or two women more in each level. The obvious source of difference is National Standard Scale and 'A' and 'B' allowance holders, where there are many more women than would follow from random distribution, and 'D' allowance holders, where there are many fewer women.

Since they gave the same amount of time to work as men, women were 'better value for money' if their work were to be considered on a strictly cost-of-the-job basis. (This view is strengthened by the evidence that women teachers spent more time teaching the (larger) Key Stage 3 classes.)

Third, we found significantly more women (p<.001) falling into the category of one to ten years of experience of secondary teaching. There were fifty-two teachers overall in this category, of whom forty-three were women. The difference here was much greater than in other categories of length of experience.

The findings here are of some interest in respect of policies for equal opportunities. We had data on the salary status, age and length of teaching experience of the teachers, both men and women. As has been shown in Table 8.1, women were over-represented in the lower salary statuses and underrepresented in the higher statuses, especially 'D' allowances. This gender difference held up when the age of teachers was taken into the analysis, but almost disappeared when, instead of age, the length of teaching experience was the basis for analysis. In effect the gender inequalities in salary status in the sample appear to be derived mainly from the consequences of the 'career break' of women teachers rather than from deliberate discrimination or from in-school obstacles to promotion for women.

Thus, the data we have presented indicate that female teachers in the schools were at a disadvantage by comparison with their male colleagues. They taught the larger classes more, and the smaller classes less, than men; they clustered more on the lower, and less on the higher, salary levels than men; and more women than men were on fixed-term contracts. There is no self-evident explanation or justification for this state of affairs. The women worked as long hours as men and spent more time on in-service training at weekends. Furthermore, there was no difference in 'conscientiousness' between men and women. The women, therefore, represented better value for money (from an employer's perspective) or an exploited group of workers (from the perspective of equal opportunities). Maclure and Marr (1990) argue that an 'underclass' of women teachers was developing in the schools and, although we would not think our evidence strong enough to support their conclusion, or at least their terminology, it does alert us to the possibility of an underclass developing.

The reasons for the relatively disadvantaged positions of women in schools are complex. In a broad-ranging analysis Al-Khalifa (1989) argues that the position for promotion and career development of women has deteriorated since Byrne's (1978) study, with 'women clustering in greater proportions on Scales 1 and 2 [equivalent to the National Standard Scale in our study] and with few signs of a reverse in this decline' (p. 83). She claims that although part of the reason is direct sex-stereotyping and sex discrimination, women's perceptions play a part also; they are more 'self-critical and selective' about promotion and more of them have to take account of responsibilities outside work. She also highlights the problem of the masculine image of school management in the symbolic order of the school life, a bias which has increased under new forms of managerialism, with its emphasis on positions such as 'chief executive'. The values of this new technicist approach can be seen as masculine, emphasising 'analytical detachment, strong task direction and hard-nosed toughness' (p. 87), according to Al-Khalifa, in what may be seen as a reverse form of sex-stereotyping itself. For these kinds of reasons women have tended to resist pressure for promotion. In an interesting aside, Al-Khalifa (1989, pp. 87–8) comments that:

> Knowledge and experience of gender-linked issues are not normally required preparation for management, and demonstrable skills in relating to women staff and girl pupils are not sought out as necessary qualities for the performance of staff and pupil management.

Our evidence is less broad in sweep than would be needed to explore all the issues associated with differences in status and career development between men and women in secondary schools. However, interestingly, in the light of the above comment, we found women staff more frequently given responsibility for pastoral care, perhaps a management responsibility seen as needing more 'feminine' qualities.

However, when length of experience was controlled, the sex differences in salary scale in our sample were substantially reduced, and we have argued that this seems to imply that a main source of discrimination against the women teachers was not within the school but outside it, arising from the 'career break' experienced by women. If true, this would not mean that a school's equal opportunity policies should be regarded as irrelevant, but that the major source of inequality cannot easily or fully be resolved by such policies. Wider social policies, especially those concerned with child-care provision, would need to be implemented for those women teachers who wish to avoid career breaks if the inequalities we found are to be removed.

Nevertheless, even without such wider policies, governing

bodies might wish to avoid the worst aspects of gender disadvantage by adopting deliberate in-school policies. These could include the monitoring of the use of fixed-term contracts in order to reduce the number of women wishing for permanent contracts being awarded fixed-term ones; the recognition of the career break as a professional advantage rather than a disadvantage, for example, by fully counting 'years of experience' related to children since training, whether or not carried out in school; and the monitoring of teaching duties to see that female teachers are not allocated disproportionate numbers of large classes, or fewer opportunities for teaching classes well matched to their background or more Key Stage 3 classes than male teachers. Some of the disadvantages experienced in work can be resolved through such mundane but effective analysis by school management.

CONCLUSION

In discussing these issues we have avoided the tendency to rush to apparently obvious and generalised conclusions, preferring instead to raise possible options for school management. However, we reiterate our basic view that analysis of the ways in which teachers' time is actually used inevitably raises questions about whether the actual use is the best use in the interests of the school, its teachers and its pupils. In a changing educational and political climate it would be strange if the current use of teachers' time were also the best use of it, and this constitutes a major challenge for those responsible for the management of the schools.

9

SECONDARY SCHOOL TEACHING UNDER IMPOSED CHANGE: SOME CONTRIBUTIONS TO THEORISING

INTRODUCTION

We have been studying the work of secondary school teachers in much of the United Kingdom as they responded to a specific set of changes imposed upon them by some of the provisions of the Education Reform Act 1988. In particular, we have been examining the effect of the imposition of the National Curriculum and RE at Key Stage 3, changes in examination and assessment practice at Key Stage 4, new patterns of vocational education post-16, and management changes introduced by the Education Reform Act, most obviously those concerned with the local management of schools. There has also been the extension of in-service training. 'Imposed' change in education is a problematic idea; all educational provision in the maintained sector is essentially imposed in the sense that it is legislated for, and logically, therefore, all *changes* in provision are *ipso facto* imposed. However, the changes to the curriculum after 1988 were imposed in one particular sense. Curriculum change before 1988 had been piecemeal and voluntary; it had depended upon the initiative of individual teachers, schools or local education authorities. These individual initiatives could draw upon development projects from major agencies such as the Schools Council or the Nuffield Foundation, but such projects had no power at the implementation stage and no right of access to the processes of teacher training at either the initial or in-service stages. Although this arrangement was superficially democratic in that it was based on assumptions of teacher and school

156

autonomy in curriculum decision-making, it was ineffective in bringing about general curriculum change (see Steadman *et al.* 1978, Salter and Tapper 1981). After 1988 curriculum change was, for all practical purposes, universal and statutory, focused upon the delivery in every school of the National Curriculum and RE. For the first time since 1944, the *de facto* autonomy in curriculum matters had been constrained by law. The constraint resided in the four components of the concept of curriculum embodied in the Education Reform Act 1988, viz., programmes of study; attainment targets divided into hierarchically structured criteria, called statements of attainment; assessment arrangements; and the ten-subject + RE framework. The four components were established in law through statutory orders providing the enforceable prescriptions by which teachers' work on the curriculum was controlled. The most direct effect on secondary schools was the difficulty it created for sustaining options at the beginning of Key Stage 4, and the requirement to teach some subjects that had previously been optional, for example a modern foreign language, to all pupils irrespective of their inclination or ability.

TEN CHARACTERISTICS OF SECONDARY TEACHERS' WORK

In the above context, the evidence about secondary teachers' work in this book can bear the following interpretations, using the average data on all the teachers irrespective of the age range taught or the status held. The data used to illustrate the interpretations have been drawn from Sample 1 only because of its relatively large numbers and wide geographical spread.

First (and despite the absence of an established baseline), teachers' workloads had increased substantially to the stage where a term-time working week of over fifty-four hours had become the norm, compared to the 46.75 recorded in 1976 by Hilsum and Strong.

Second, the patterning of teachers' time had been restructured, with at least 59 per cent of their time being spent out of contact with pupils, and only 41 per cent at most being spent in contact with them. Teaching, strictly defined, took less than a third of teachers' working time and about 68 per cent of the minimum time notionally available for teaching in the week, viz., twenty-five hours per week.

Third, with the exception of deputy heads and 'C' allowance holders, the accumulation of responsibilities and salary incentives did not generally affect the amount of time spent on work (although it did affect the nature of the work itself). The main influence on the amount of time spent was the personal sense of 'conscientiousness' (see Chapter 3).

Of the time they spent teaching, 15 per cent was spent teaching subjects for which they were not qualified by their initial training.

Fifth, a substantial proportion of teachers' time, about 14 per cent of the working week, was spent on administration for the school and in connection with examinations. An unknown quantity of this time was spent on low-level activities which could, in principle, be carried out by para-professionals. The proportions of time on all administration varied from 7 per cent (National Standard Scale) to 35 per cent (deputy heads).

Sixth, time spent on teaching in relation to preparing could be typically expressed as a ratio of 1:0.8, although it should be remembered that the latter included marking and recording results as well as planning lessons and organising resources.

Seventh, compared to the primary teachers we studied (see Campbell and Neill 1994), secondary teachers spent their time less intensively, with relatively little time in 'simultaneous working', i.e., carrying out two or more activities at the same time. This was true for work overall, where the '105 per cent workload' is shown for Sample 1 in Table 3.3 in Chapter 3. They did little simultaneous teaching of different subjects, with nearly all teaching being single subject in nature. (They operated a '104 per cent curriculum' (taking both samples into account) compared to the primary teachers' '200 per cent curriculum'.) They had more non-contact time and smaller classes than primary teachers.

Eighth, work carried over into break times, with nearly 50 per cent of break times being used for work.

Ninth, the work of teaching was relatively isolated from other adults, with 68 per cent of teachers having no time with another teacher in their class, and only 13 per cent having an assistant or technician with them for some time in the week. However, teachers' work overall involved professional collaboration and/

or contact with colleagues. Over four-and-a-half hours a week were spent in meetings, non-pupil days, inter-school liaison and in-service training, all in the company of, and interacting professionally with, teacher colleagues.

Tenth, a substantial proportion (27 per cent) of teachers' work was invisible to the public, carried out at home in the evenings and at weekends. As we have shown in Table 3.5 in Chapter 3, teachers spent just under forty hours a week at school but, in addition, fourteen-and-a-half hours a week were spent on work off school premises, of which over six hours were spent at weekends.

The detailed data that made up this overall picture have been provided in previous chapters and enable us to comment upon some particular theories about teachers' work. These are the related theories of 'intensification' and 'de-professionalisation' or 'de-skilling'.

'Intensification' refers to the pressure on teachers to do more work than previously in the same time – to improve productivity; 'de-skilling'/'de-professionalisation' refers to the pressure on teachers to implement the ideas of others, whereas previously they generated the ideas that they implemented. In addition, under 'de-skilling', some skills carried out by teachers can be carried out by other adults, at lower cost. In commenting on them we are simply intending to show where our evidence supports theory or appears to contradict it. We do not attempt a full-scale critique of the theories themselves, which would need fuller treatment than is available here.

INTENSIFICATION OF TEACHERS' WORK

The 'intensification' thesis is traceable to the ideas of an American sociologist (Larson 1980) who argued that professional non-manual workers – 'educated labour' as he called them – experienced, under late twentieth-century capitalism, increased pressure for productivity and efficiency in their work. This had resulted in reduced collegial relations, less time for relaxation in official breaks and deterioration in the quality of the service they provided as corners were cut. The thesis was applied to the position of teachers by Apple (1986) in a neo-Marxist analysis published as *Teachers and Texts*. Apple argued that intensification 'represents one of the most tangible ways in which the work privileges of educational workers are eroded'. It ranged from the apparently trivial – not being allowed a coffee break – to having a 'total absence of time to keep up with one's field' and the 'chronic sense of work overload' (p. 41). In education, according to Apple, the process was especially clear in schools dominated by 'behaviourally pre-specified curricula, repeated testing, and strict and reductive accountability systems' (p. 43). In particular, Apple cited one school where teachers spent increasingly large amounts of time in setting and marking test material, administrating the material and implementing pre-specified curriculum activities. Under curricular systems like this, 'getting done' (i.e., getting through all the work) replaced quality teaching in the teachers' objectives.

In an extension to the argument (Apple and Jungck 1991), Apple argued, on the basis of a study of two elementary teachers who had introduced a computer-based mathematics programme in their classes, that the elementary teachers had less time for the affective aspects of their relationships with the pupils because of time spent on assessment and bureaucratic tasks.

Where teacher resistance to the intensification of their work occurred, it took the form of subverting some of the curricular objectives, or deliberately finding time in the day for less pressurised activities. Nonetheless, in order to deliver the curriculum the teachers had to acquire new technical and managerial skills, and tended to see this as increased professionalism. Moreover, because of their tendency, voluntarily, to take on more work than was contractually necessary, teachers seemed to be colluding in their own intensification. Linking his argument to analyses of class and gender relations, Apple rejected the teachers' perceptions of their own increased professionalism, saying that they 'mis-recognised' the intensification process and its inevitable de-skilling. In effect, he took the view that the teachers were guilty of operating in a false consciousness. The intensification thesis was taken up with varying degrees of critical scepticism by English writers (Lee 1987, Ozga and Lawn 1988, Ozga 1988, Lawn and Grace 1987) who emphasised the 'de-professionalisation' and 'proletarianisation' of teachers.

Lawn and Ozga (1988), who have contributed significantly to theorising on proletarianisation in education, noted, in what they described as a 'tentative thesis', that there was 'a connection between the increased proletarianisation of teachers' work, de-skilling and re-skilling, and "class-in-itself" actions of teachers' (p. 87). They acknowledged that they had to argue by inference from the position of other workers who, under the changing nature of capitalism, are seen as in the process of proletarianisation. Lawn and Ozga define this as following from:

> the removal of skill from work, the exclusion of the worker from the conceptual functions of work. Worker autonomy is eroded, the relationship between employer and employee breaks down, management controls are strengthened and craft skills and the craft ethic decline . . . . If education is part of the creation of value, expressed as a trained work force, then this process will be analysed and restructured to increase its efficiency (productivity).
>
> (Lawn and Ozga 1988, pp. 87–8)

Lawn and Ozga cite Braverman (1974) to the effect that there was now a long-term process of de-skilling in train, whereby workers lose craft and traditional abilities, but also lose out because knowledge progressively becomes diffused through the production process. The consequence was that workers previously enjoying distinctive skills could now be replaced more cheaply by those with lower skills.

Both perspectives, intensification and proletarianisation, seemed particularly applicable to the politics of education after 1988, since the curriculum and assessment reforms obviously required teachers to implement a curriculum invented by others and imposed upon all maintained-sector schools; under devolved budgets there was a growth of managerialism, the main objectives of which were to increase efficiency and to control costs at the level of the individual school.

There are three great difficulties in attempting to test the intensification thesis as applied to education by Apple. The first is an historical one. It is not self-evident that contemporary secondary teachers' work has been intensified compared to, say, teachers in the early part of the twentieth century, where typically they had very large class groups and skill levels not associated with professional status. Likewise, compared to teachers in the early post-war secondary modern schools, it is uncertain that intensification has occurred. Furthermore, in the

United States in the first twenty years of this century, pressures to improve productivity at the expense of quality – very similar to those operating now – were put upon teachers (see Callahan 1962). In this country, before 1926, teachers operated under regulations that gave them little professional autonomy in curriculum matters. If intensification means that teachers are doing more work in the same time-frame, or that they are required more to implement others' curricula and create their own less, a fundamental question, unanswered by Apple, is: 'More than when?'.

Second, the conflation of the concept of intensification with that of de-skilling makes it difficult to envisage a workplace culture where one might occur without the other. Yet this is exactly what Osborn and Broadfoot (1991) and ourselves (Campbell *et al.* 1991) reported about primary teachers' implementation of the National Curriculum, with teachers clearly feeling both intensification of their work and the simultaneous enhancement of their professional skills. Acker's work (1987, 1992) supports this interpretation.

The third problem is the assumed correspondence in Larson's analysis, although not necessarily Apple's, between intensification and late twentieth-century capitalist economies. Unfortunately, by the last decade of the century there are, excepting China, so few non-capitalist economies left that it would be difficult to find appropriate bases for cross-cultural comparison. Nonetheless, cross-cultural analyses of teachers' work (International Labour Office 1981, 1991) stress the close resemblances in teachers' work rather than differences according to political economy. ILO (1981) pointed out the tendency to underestimate teacher workloads and intensity in both developing and industrialised countries. Sweden, which has had one of the most socialist/welfare-oriented economies in the industrialised world, is cited as an example by ILO (1991, p. 84) of increasing intensification as teachers take on more moral and social responsibilities, previously held by families, communities and churches. And the highest number of specified hours per week (42.5) in industrialised countries (in 1988) was for the then communist Czechoslovakia, followed by the strongly capitalist Singapore (ILO 1991, Table X, p. 85). The study by Paine (1990) of Chinese teachers' conceptions of time between 1982 and 1987 reported that teachers serving as *banzhuren* (class advisers) worked long hours, 'often going from 6.00a.m. to after 5.00p.m.' (p. 145), that teachers worked a six-day week and that 'many teachers suffer from exhaustion, fatigue and depression' (p. 146).

Although, as has been said, comparisons are difficult, given that the ILO data relied on secondary sources, the superficial picture does not suggest that a greater intensification is distinctly associated with capitalist economies.

The thesis also runs into the difficulty that studies show that the basic and actual hours of work of both manual and non-manual workers have steadily decreased over the century, and that the emerging model in a 'post-Fordist' occupational culture is for both educated and less educated labour to negotiate and control their hours of work more flexibly to suit their individual needs (see Hewitt 1993, Price and Bain 1988, New Earnings Survey 1991, Marsh 1991).

The Apple thesis has been tested against specific empirical realities by Hargreaves (1991) and Acker (1990, 1992). Both writers found Apple's treatment of teachers' perceptions as 'misrecognition', 'demeaning' to the teachers and 'churlish', with Acker (1992) simply stating that, for her primary teachers, introducing the National Curriculum had not led to de-skilling as they saw it: 'Their enhanced skill feels real to them and looks real to me' (p. 270). The evidence from Volume 2 in this series (Evans *et al.* (1994)) supports Acker's view strongly, but we think a more important logical point needs to be made about Apple's treatment of the teachers' views. Even accepting Ozga and Lawn's (1988) argument that skill is a contested concept, if any view from the world of classrooms, contradicting the general intensification thesis, is to be seen as simply derived from false consciousness, the thesis itself cannot be subject to falsification, and therefore ceases to be interesting to researchers.

In a sustained critical analysis of the intensification thesis, Hargreaves (1991) drew out what he described as the 'propositions within the intensification thesis' as a starting point for subjecting the thesis to the empirical realities of an investigation he had conducted into the use of contractually negotiated 'preparation time' guaranteed to elementary teachers in most of Ontario's school boards. The teachers had gone on strike in 1987 in support of a claim for 180 minutes per week of preparation time. By 1991 they had a guaranteed minimum of 120 minutes preparation time per week, and the way they used this time was the focus of Hargreaves's investigation. In particular, the impact of such guaranteed provision of time upon the individualistic culture of primary schools, and the extent to which it supported collaboration and a more collaborative culture, was of particular interest to Hargreaves. The investigation used interviews with twelve principals and twenty-eight teachers in twelve schools in two school boards. The eight propositions Hargreaves elicited were as follows:

1 intensification leads to reduced time for relaxation;
2 intensification leads to lack of time to keep up with one's field;
3 intensification reduces opportunities for interaction with colleagues;
4 intensification creates chronic work overload that fosters dependency on outside experts;
5 intensification reduces the quality of service by encouraging 'cutting of corners';
6 intensification leads to diversification of responsibility and, with it, heightened dependency on experts;
7 intensification creates and reinforces scarcities of preparation time; and
8 intensification is voluntarily supported by many teachers and misrecognised as professionalism.

(Hargreaves 1991, p. 5)

This reformulation by Hargreaves is a considerable advance for purposes of empirical testing of the intensification thesis as it was formulated by Apple. Nonetheless, there are problems with it. Propositions 4, 5, 6, 7 and 8 are all, in effect, dual propositions in which there is no logical or necessary connection between the first and second parts. For example, in respect of the fourth proposition, you could have chronic workload without dependency on outside experts. Likewise, in the fifth proposition, cutting corners might not lead to reduced quality of service. Moreover, some key ambiguities remain in the British policy context from the mid-1980s onwards. What meanings are to be attached to 'keeping up with one's field' in a period that has seen the development of increased earmarked funding for in-service training of teachers, but only for the realisation of central government's objectives? The 'field' has been redefined for many subject teachers and for those with management responsibilities in secondary schools, as well as those responsible for providing vocationally oriented courses at the post-16 stage. Paradoxically from the point of view of the second proposition, part of the increase in workload is attributable to a frantic scurrying to understand and keep up with one's field. The time available, in the sense of funded in-service training time with supply cover to replace teaching time, to keep up with the newly defined fields has increased, and may be seen as *contributing* to intensification of work, not being hindered by it.

Equally, what counts as 'dependency on outside experts' for British teachers in a period where they have had fewer opportunities to be dependent for accreditation upon higher education institutions? With some financial autonomy to buy in-service training according to the school's definitions of their needs, and a statutory framework of five non-pupil days in which most professional development has been designed by the school staff, added to the exercise of 'consumer power' through the schools' control of budgets for professional development, there is no prima facie case for assuming an increase in dependency on outside experts. On the contrary, for most schools the activities of the non-pupil days are defined by the school teachers, often according to a development plan negotiated in staff meetings and led by members of the school staff.

The evidence in this book relates in the main to the first three propositions, since they are primarily concerned with the use of teachers' time. (In addition, the evidence in Volume 2 of this series (Evans *et al.* (1994)) relates to the element of 'chronic work overload' in the fourth proposition.) All three suffer from (the first and third explicitly, the second by implication) the lack of an historical baseline, as mentioned earlier and acknowledged by Hargreaves. Second, although it is not entirely clear, it seems from Apple's work that the relaxation and interaction with colleagues refer only to time in the school day, not outside it – a rather narrow way of conceiving the issue. With these reservations in mind we may draw upon our evidence.

First, the time for relaxation in the school day may be examined by the use of time during official breaks and non-contact time. For our teachers, the former includes the time allocated for morning coffee break (typically some fifteen to twenty minutes), lunchtime (typically some sixty to seventy-five minutes) and, where it occurred, afternoon break (similar to the morning coffee break). As we have shown in Chapter 6, our teachers had, in total, a little over three hours a week in breaks free of work. In respect of non-contact time, although formally allocated well over three hours per week, in practice just under half-an-hour a week of it was used for relaxation (see Table 6.1 in Chapter 6). Whether these two pieces of empirical evidence show *reduced* relaxation time in the school day, against some unspecified baseline in the past, is uncertain, but they do indirectly support the underlying argument of the first of Hargreaves's reformulations about intensification, since they show that our teachers enjoyed much less time in the school day for relaxation than the amount they were officially allocated for non-contact time, and in relation to breaks to which they were statutorily entitled.

The evidence about time to keep up with one's field comprises, in our study, time spent on professional development, which included time on courses, conferences, etc., travel to them, meetings, including staff meetings, and non-pupil days. There are difficulties in deciding how much of this time should count as contributing to professional development and thus helping teachers keep up with their field.

If we take the minimum time, i.e., courses, conferences, travel to them and non-pupil days, the amount of time per week was just over two hours, or 4 per cent of teachers' working week. If we take the maximum time of just under five-and-a-half hours, the proportion rises to 10 per cent of the teachers' working week.

There are two conclusions about this evidence. First, compared to time spent on professional development by teachers in Hilsum and Strong's (1978) study, even the minimum time spent by our teachers shows an increase. This is to be expected given the earmarking of in-service training grants in the late 1980s compared to their absence in the 1960s/1970s, but in any case does not support the aspect of the intensification thesis embodied in Hargreaves's second proposition. Second, and in contrast, our overall evidence shows teachers working nearly fifty-five hours a week in term-time. This is an increase of about eight hours over Hilsum and Strong's teachers which, by definition, eats into teachers' own time and therefore reduces the time available for reading, course participation and for following courses leading to further qualifications. In this sense, the intensification thesis would be supported. That the same aspect of the thesis can be both not supported and supported by the *same evidence* is perhaps an indication of the vagueness of its original formulation.

It also needs to be added that, compared to Hilsum and Strong's teachers fifteen years ago, more time for professional development has been funded, and the funds earmarked, and more control over the funds has passed to the schools themselves. However, more professional development time for our teachers will be spent on institutionally determined objectives rather than individually determined ones.

The third formulation links intensification to reduced time for interaction with colleagues. Our evidence here is limited to the time spent working with colleagues as opposed to mixing informally with them in breaks, lunchtimes and on other occasions. It applies, therefore, to a limited concept of interaction with colleagues. Two points emerge from our evidence. The first is that, in general, the amount of collaborative working, including both working with other adults in the classroom and in professional meetings outside it, is substantial, amounting to about 10 per cent of the working week and an increase on Hilsum and Strong's teachers. Second, the more senior the staff, as has been shown in Chapter 5, the more time was spent in interaction with colleagues (to include meetings, and all sub-categories of professional development except professional reading). In the sense we have defined it above, therefore, increased interaction with colleagues, compared to the position some fifteen years ago, characterised the work of teachers in our study.

One further point arises from our evidence in relation to Lawn and Ozga's (1988) analysis of de-skilling, outlined above. It is possible to interpret our evidence as supporting the idea that, for senior teachers at least, de-skilling is occurring since they spend, as has been argued in Chapter 8, considerable amounts of their time on work of a relatively low skill level. The paradox here is that de-skilling in this sense occurs as teachers are promoted and move into work taking them away from classroom teaching, the activity arguably requiring the clearest and most distinctively professional exercise of skill by those employed as teachers of subjects in secondary schools. However, this aspect of de-skilling, we would argue, sits uneasily with the intensification thesis, which explains the changes in teachers' work relations largely by reference to increased pressure for efficiency and productivity. Currently, the shift of such time allocation to tasks outside the classroom leads to lower productivity in terms of fewer pupils taught. However, if the argument advanced in Chapter 8 becomes adopted by school management and low-level tasks currently carried out by senior staff are redistributed through the appointment of more clerical and administrative staff, Ozga and Lawn's analysis might be confirmed.

CONCLUSION

We reiterate that we have not been subjecting the grand theories of intensification and de-skilling to comprehensive critiques. Our more modest aim has been to see where, if at all, our evidence bears upon such theories. In general, we have been helped in this aim by the reformulation of Hargreaves (1991) and, if his reformulations are accepted, our evidence casts doubt on some aspects of the theorising. As is often the case with theory construction in education, more evidence and more empirical research would be helpful.

10

THE DILEMMA OF TEACHER CONSCIENTIOUSNESS

We have shown in Part I of this book the pervasive influence of teachers' sense of 'conscientiousness' upon their working hours. We measured 'conscientiousness' by teachers' response to one (rather lengthily expressed) item on the questionnaire. The item (Item 2.6), which included a near verbatim quotation from the Teachers' Pay and Conditions Document (Interim Advisory Committee 1990), defining non-directed time, read:

> It has been assumed that, in order to perform their professional duties during the school day (i.e., teaching, supervision, assembly, registration, staff meetings and other 'directed' time) teachers will need to spend an unspecified amount of time preparing for such duties in their own 'non-directed' time. As a general rule, and excluding holidays, how many hours a week do you think it is reasonable for you to be expected to spend in non-directed time (i.e., mainly planning, record-keeping, report-writing, organising resources, keeping up-to-date, and all INSET)?

The teachers had to respond by indicating the amount of time they thought was reasonable, choosing from five-hour ranges spreading from 'none' to 'over 30 hours'. As can be seen from Table 10.1, the responses ranged from one–five hours to twenty-six–thirty hours, with the majority of teachers (86 per cent) answering either one–five, six–ten or eleven–fifteen hours. Taking the mid-point of each range, and ignoring the 'missing' category, the average reasonable expectation for non-directed time was 9.3 hours per week.

We can conclude that the teachers, in general, thought it was reasonable for them to be expected to work no more than ten

Table 10.1 Teacher perceptions of reasonable expectations for non-directed time

Reasonable expectations (hours per week)	Number of teachers	% teachers
None	13	3
1–5	61	16
6–10	168	44
11–15	99	26
16–20	27	7
21–25	8	2
26–30	1	0
Above 30	0	0
Missing	7	2
Total	384	100

hours in their 'own' time during the term-time weeks, which, added to the thirty-three hours of directed time, would give a term-time working week of forty-three hours. With any work carried out in vacations ignored, this would give annual hours of forty-three hours × thirty-eight weeks + one week of non-pupil days at thirty hours = 1,664 hours annually. Assuming vacations and public holidays amount to six weeks a year, the hours that the teachers considered as reasonable for them to be expected to work were equivalent to a thirty-six-hour working week spread across forty-six weeks of the year, and would approximate to the typical pattern of a basic thirty-seven-hour working week for non-manual workers nationally (see Incomes Data Services 1992). As we have shown in Chapter 3, the actual hours worked by the teachers were some eleven hours per week (and over 400 hours per year) more than the teachers considered reasonable. For every hour of directed time, the teachers worked 0.61 hours (nearly forty minutes) in their own 'non-directed' time.

We have labelled teachers' responses to Item 2.6 on the questionnaire as 'conscientiousness' for two reasons: we wanted to signify something of the vocational motivation - of the personal and moral sense of obligation – represented by their answers; and we wanted a term that could embody not only the virtue of vocational motivation but also the idea that teachers could spend too much of their own time on work, as might be implied by the use of the term 'over-conscientiousness', or 'conscientious to a fault'. For this reason, 'conscientiousness' as we use it here, implies not so much value approval as value ambivalence. In using the term 'conscientiousness' we have, for this item only, deliberately deviated from our decision, referred to in Chapter 1, to use morally neutral terminology. This is because we believe that the item actually represented a moral (or, at the very least, personal) dimension to teacher motivation.

THE INFLUENCE OF 'CONSCIENTIOUSNESS' UPON TEACHERS' WORK

For the next stage in this argument, we have assumed that there is some degree of validity in using responses to this one questionnaire item as an indicator of conscientiousness – a matter to which we return later in this chapter – and now provide a summary of the relationship between conscientiousness and the amount of time spent on work. The summary is for conscientiousness and aspects of work associated with it, in Sample 1.

Table 10.2 Association between 'conscientiousness' and categories of work

Category	Significance of trend
Total time on work – on school premises	(p<.001)
Total time on work – weekdays	(p<.001)
Total work – on school premises	(p<.05)
Total work – off school premises	(p<.001)
Preparation and professional development combined	(p<.01)
Preparation	(p<.001)
Preparation – weekdays	(p<.01)
Preparation – on school premises	(p<.01)
Preparation – for Key Stage 3	(p<.01)
Lesson planning	(p<.05)
Lesson planning – on school premises	(p<.05)
Lesson planning – weekdays	(p<.05)
Marking	(p<.05)
Organising resources, etc.	(p<.05)
Organising resources, etc. – weekdays	(p<.01)
Professional development – off school premises	(p<.05)
Travel to in-service courses – off school premises	(p<.05)
Working breaks	(p<.05)
Pastoral care	(p<.05)

Conscientiousness was positively associated (linear trend) with the time spent on work overall and on aspects of work, either in combination or separately. The associations were as above, and were for time spent on all days on and off school premises combined, unless otherwise stated.

It can be seen from the above summary how pervasive an influence on these teachers conscientiousness was; it affected total time spent on work and most pervasively – and the source of many of the statistical differences – affected time spent on preparation, both overall and in its separate aspects of lesson planning, marking and organising. The statistical strength of the trends was, in general, greater for time spent off school premises, i.e., in the teachers' own time. The strength of the association with total time spent on work is clear from the summary above but is, nonetheless, understated. We have followed convention in reporting the probability of the association occurring by chance as smaller than one in a thousand ($p < .001$). In fact, the probabilities for total time, total time on weekdays and total time off school premises were smaller than one in ten thousand ($p < .0001$).

In addition to total time and preparation, there was a weak trend in the relationship between conscientiousness and time spent on professional development off school premises, and interestingly in the amount of break time spent on work. Teachers with higher levels of conscientiousness also spent more time on aspects of pastoral care with individual pupils, irrespective of whether they had an allowance for pastoral care.

Two points may be made about the above pattern. The first is that if our assumption about the questionnaire item by which 'conscientiousness' was measured had good validity, the pattern is largely as might be expected: overall time on work would be associated with high conscientiousness and those aspects of work most subject to the discretion of the individual teacher, viz., preparation and its sub-categories – markedly those carried out away from the school premises, i.e., in the teachers' own time – would be the ones most influenced by it. The evidence about professional development, working breaks and pastoral care is also congruent with our assumption. We had expected that time on extra-curricular activities such as sports, orchestras and field trips, etc., would also be associated with conscientiousness, but this was not the case.

172

Second, there was no general association between 'conscientiousness' and salary status, except that deputy heads had significantly higher levels of conscientiousness than other teachers. Long hours on work generally were associated not with *positional* characteristics of the job, such as responsibilities, allowances or status in the school hierarchy, but with a *personal* characteristic of the teacher, viz., their own sense of what it was reasonable for the education system to expect of them. Like their primary school counterparts, these secondary school teachers were more motivated by a sense of their work as a vocation than by contractual characteristics, at least in terms of the amount of their 'own' time they were prepared to devote to it.

THE PROBLEM WITH CONSCIENTIOUSNESS

We would not wish to detract from the value of teachers' vocational attachment to work, or from the strong professional identity that secondary teachers create from extensive commitment to their work. Teachers' professional responsibilities are more diffuse than simply the transmission of subject knowledge since they include a sense of responsibility not merely for cognitive goals but also for social, emotional and personal well-being. This diffuse responsibility has been encouraged, expected or required in a long train of official and semi-official documents, at least since the 1960s (e.g., White Paper 1985) and stretching beyond the legislation of the 1980s (White Paper 1992, Chapter 8).

It is easy to see why diffuse responsibilities characterise secondary teaching. Secondary teachers are dealing with young people at a difficult time in their lives, the relationship between the school and occupational destinies is fairly direct and contemporary schools have to take on greater social and emotional responsibilities as the authority of family, church, law and other community support structures weakens (International Labour Office 1991). Social imperatives drive teachers towards an ethic of care, often institutionalised into formal arrangements for the provision of counselling, pastoral care and careers advice. Alternative perspectives (e.g., Cox and Dyson 1969, 1970) have seen debased versions of concerns for pupils' social welfare becoming a substitute for cognitive objectives. There is a tendency to romanticise the caring ethic, and even, in Fullan and

Hargreaves (1991), to polarise it against an ethic of respon-sibility. Yet we would argue that the ethic of care as a central value in teachers' occupational culture contributes to work overload.

INFLATING EXPECTATIONS

As we have shown above, one set of role expectations is that teachers meet the social and emotional needs of their pupils. Whilst this has been a constant feature of their role in western countries (see International Labour Office 1991), in England and Wales the recent trends in legislation have added to, or exten-ded, three other elements. The most obvious is that the curri-culum requirements have made more public and more stringent expectations for pupils' cognitive achievement. There has also been the introduction of a powerful drive to 'market account-ability' (Troman 1989), through the publication of end-of-Key Stage test results, open enrolment policies, and the funding of schools being based largely on pupil numbers. Thus the teachers previously able to insulate themselves from concerns about whole-school development and to concentrate energies upon the needs of the subject departments and the pupils in the class now have to take account of the implications of their work for the whole school, and especially its market image, mediated largely through the reporting of pupil achievement in end-of-year or end-of-Key Stage reporting.

Third, even the most junior teachers spend time on aspects of management or administration. Managing aspects of the work of other teachers is part of the contractual obligation of all teachers. Thus, the obligations and expectations now form an expanded and tri-cornered accountability: to pupils' welfare, to the curriculum and to their colleagues and school.

This inflation of work demands impacts upon domestic and personal life. Conventionally the problem has been seen as affecting married female teachers. For example, Evetts (1990) noted that, 'Women teachers will have responsibilities in at least two spheres: the public sphere of work and the private sphere of home and family' (p. 115). She added that the difficulty of fulfilling work and family commitments became 'particularly acute' when there were children in the family, but also drew attention to the emerging demographic factor of increasing numbers of dependent elderly relatives whose care often falls disproportionately upon the shoulders of women.

In this context it should be noted that, in a study of 3,019 primary and secondary teachers, Varlaam *et al.* (1992) found few differences in rank order of factors affecting morale and motivation, but 'having sufficient time for family and private life' was more important amongst married teachers than others. (Although there is a sense in which this finding states the obvious, since married teachers are more likely to have more substantial family commitments than unmarried ones, the fact that it is obvious does not mean that it is not a real force on teachers.) 'Married' in the Varlaam *et al.* study did not relate to female teachers exclusively, but there were differences between men and women in sources of dissatisfaction, more men reporting dissatisfaction with pay, workload, physical environment and opportunities to use skills. However, commonalities rather than differences characterised male and female teachers generally.

Varlaam and his colleagues found that by far the commonest unsatisfactory factors in the teachers' present post and current circumstances were those relating to stress, excessive workloads, paperwork and record-keeping, inadequate resources and insufficient time for family and private life. These findings are not surprising, but such dissatisfactions are likely to be particularly salient for female teachers, for whom there are the added demands arising from what Sharpe (1984) has called the 'Double Identity'. (See also Hewitt 1993 for an extended discussion of women's working hours.)

TOWARDS THE CONTROL OF CONSCIENTIOUSNESS

When the special position of female teachers has been acknowledged, the evidence from Varlaam and his colleagues was that workload and stress were seen as a general problem. For example, irrespective of gender, salary status or school type, teachers in their study placed 'reduced working time outside school hours' as the second-ranked most important factor for teacher morale and motivation (see 1992, Table 27, p. 40). It was ranked as less important than 'more positive portrayal of the teaching profession in the media', but more important, especially by those on National Standard Scale, than 'improving pay for all teachers'.

The overall picture, therefore, is of teachers working long hours to meet increased work demands, motivated by a conscientious sense of obligation to pupils, but seeing the workloads that flow from it as a major source of low morale and motivation. In addition, for some teachers heavy teaching loads are a major source of stress (Kyriacou 1980).

The demands on teachers could either become manageable or be seen clearly as unmanageable if the inflation of their role were limited by contractual bounds. But the demands were being inflated in a contractual framework that was itself – because of the way 'non-directed' time was defined – literally without limit. Indeed, part of the definition – 'such additional hours as may be necessary to enable them to discharge effectively their professional duties' (Department of Education and Science 1989a, para. 36(1)(f)) – seemed to assume that if professional duties were to be increased, as they had been, the non-directed time would simply have to follow suit. It embodied an open-ended commitment of teachers' own time to work.

Within this context, 'conscientiousness', whatever its benefits to the pupils, has acted as a mechanism, actual or potential, for exploitation of teachers. Driven by their sense of obligation to meet all work demands to the best of their ability, the majority of teachers found themselves devoting much longer hours in their own time to work than they considered reasonable, and attempting to meet too many demands simultaneously in order to achieve externally defined objectives for educational reform. This was despite the fact that some of the demands – for example, those concerning the provision of a broad and balanced curriculum – were structurally impossible and have had to be revised before they were fully implemented (see National Curriculum Council/SEAC 1993). Others, such as those concerned with National Curriculum assessment at 14 and 16, were confused and unworkable.

There are three issues raised by the strength of the influence of 'conscientiousness' upon teachers' work. First, even though they were operating within a framework which, from the mid-1980s onwards in Britain, had been gradually constructed so as to impose legally binding, contractually defined duties upon teachers, and which had included the development of systems of appraisal and performance-related pay, the teachers were primarily motivated by a sense of vocation or obligation to their pupils. With the exception of the deputy heads, salary status was not associated statistically with the amount of time spent on work. The occupational culture of the school remained stubbornly at odds with the assumptions of the central government's legislation on working conditions, and especially with the intended impact of performance-related pay.

The second conclusion is that 'conscientiousness can damage your health'. Along with social work, teaching was found to be the most stressful of the professional occupations in the Oxford Employment Life survey (Gallie and White 1993). Long hours devoted to work reduced the opportunities for leisure outside schools and relaxation in school, and ate into the personal and domestic lives of our teachers. The average term-time working week was fifty-four-plus hours, a situation most saw as unreasonable. It is unlikely, as Fullan and Hargreaves (1991) argue, that anyone other than the teachers themselves will take steps to reduce work overload, since most of the overload is in the teachers' own time. The publication of two official reports indicating that the National Curriculum was not deliverable or, where it was, depth in learning was sacrificed to superficial coverage (National Curriculum Council 1993, OFSTED 1993) should give teachers the grounds, permission or excuse for acknowledging that they have been required to attempt to do the impossible, and thus to restrain their inclination to conscientiousness.

The third conclusion applies particularly to those charged with managing the schools, which includes managing the teachers. A major function for heads and other managers in the post-Education Reform Act period might be to find ways to limit teacher workloads by identifying priorities for their schools, and filtering out demands which make the most conscientious teachers' workloads unreasonable. Acker (1987) claimed that the mixture of vocationally driven motivation and high workloads amongst elementary school teachers in the United States led to 'burn-out', especially amongst female teachers. It might be worth head teachers' bearing in mind the point we made at the end of Chapter 1. There is no evidence that very long hours on work lead to better quality of teaching. Although we would not wish to be read as arguing against the vocational element in teachers' motivation, we hope that its dangers may be recognised by head teachers, and not least by the teachers themselves.

APPENDIX
Methods of data analysis

PRIMARY ANALYSIS – DATA PREPARATION

Both questionnaire and diary data were entered on to primary files using a digitising tablet; for the diary data this was supplemented by entering the teachers' hand-written codes manually, the digitiser giving the time-scale. Questionnaire data were cast directly into SPSSX data file format. The primary files for the diary data consisted of four pairs of rows per day. Each pair of rows covered four- or five-hour periods; recording started at 07.00 and finished at 24.00. One row of each pair covered activities in school, the other out-of-school activities. Within a row, a period of activity was delimited by its start and end times, with two-letter codes indicating the one or more activities occurring. Periods without school activity were left blank. Dates were entered for checking purposes, and an indication of when a day was a weekend to allow separate analysis of weekdays and weekends.

A critical point in all the diary records is that the recording system required teachers to enter all codes which occurred within a given activity period. We did not request teachers who were engaged in more than one activity simultaneously to indicate when they switched from teaching to testing within a lesson, for example; this would have been too much of a burden. Whilst we discussed the possibility of splitting a session equally between activities (for example, if a teacher spent an hour teaching two subjects simultaneously, allocating them thirty minutes each in our records) we did not feel we could make such judgements with certainty. Our system therefore more closely resembles the teacher's timetabled activity

178

than her second-to-second activity. This will especially be the case during teaching periods, when rapid switches between activities are possible. When the teacher is out of contact with children, for example at a meeting or reading, our data show more single activities in which the recorded activity will be a closer approximation to the actual activity.

PRIMARY ANALYSIS – DATA TRANSFORMATION

The primary analysis program produced a SPSSX data file in which each individual teacher's questionnaire data were combined with the appropriate data totals from her diary, and a matching SPSSX analysis file which combined category names from a master file of SPSSX commands for the questionnaire items and a file of category definitions for the diary items. The latter file was also used for the data file; it defined the components of simple and composite categories, the latter being categories such as total teaching time. Five matched pairs of files were created, one for each of the main work categories and one for other and combined activities, such as total work. These pairs of files could be run immediately under SPSSX.

The primary analysis program first checked for coding errors – illicit codes, times and numbers of rows per day. The duration of each activity was then totalled from the start and end times of each occurrence.

Composite categories were of two main types. In most cases the category was scored if any of a given set of activities were occurring in a period (i.e., an 'or' score; any of A or B or C). In some cases, such as the category for the total of teaching different subjects, the different activities tended to co-occur, so that the time spent in the composite category might not greatly exceed that for the individual categories. In others, such as 'supervision + registration + worship', the individual activities tended to be alternatives, so that the composite category approached the total of the individual categories. In a minority of cases the composite category was scored only if two activities co-occurred (i.e., an 'and' score; only if A and B coincided). In this case A and B were often 'or' combinations, e.g., the composite category was the co-occurrence of any teaching code and any preparation code.

Where appropriate, separate totals were made for weekdays,

weekends, time on and off school premises and for combinations of these.

SECONDARY ANALYSIS

Descriptive statistics, including histograms (although the figures in this book were prepared with Microsoft Chart) and inferential statistics were calculated using SPSSX. The rationale of the individual analyses is discussed in Chapter 2. Analyses of variance were performed using MEANS with the test of linearity option. Cross-tabulations were performed using CROSSTABS with the chi-square option. Factor analyses were performed using FACTOR, using Varimax rotation. The number of factors to be used was decided with the aid of a scree plot. Multiple regressions were performed using REGRESSION, with forward entry of predictors. A preliminary check to eliminate predictors which were too highly correlated was made with CORRELA-TION. Wilcoxon tests, and Kruskall-Wallis non-parametric analyses of variance for initial analyses of the smaller samples, were performed using NONPAR TESTS. In this book we have presented parametric analyses of variance for all samples, although some samples are on the small side for this purpose. The two sets of analyses of the same samples gave virtually identical results; where there were differences they related to small groups within the samples, which we discarded in any case, as explained in Chapter 2.

INDICATORS OF RELIABILITY AND VALIDITY

Self-recording systems, such as that used in this research for 'recording' the time data, are not self-evidently reliable, since those involved in the recording do so in conditions that do not allow the collection of interobserver reliability data. Moreover, volunteers may have motives that are different from non-volunteers; for example, they may wish to exaggerate their workloads for political purposes. (The diary records were sub-mitted anonymously so that personal interest could not be served by exaggerating the workload.) Such problems of reliability cannot be completely eradicated in self-recording systems, but some internal checks can be made.

In this study we included three items on the questionnaire

that served this purpose. Teachers were asked to say whether the time overall they spent on work in the recorded week was about the same, more or less than in other weeks in the term, and whether time spent on professional development was about the same, more or less. They were also asked to 'estimate' whether their workloads had increased since the same time last year. In response to this last question almost no teachers said it had reduced, and we therefore could not use these answers to test internal reliability. However, for the other two items it was possible. Those teachers who said they spent about the same time or less in previous weeks on work compared to the recorded week, actually recorded more time on the respective items in the recorded week – we came to know this as 'truthful reporting'.

Likewise, those saying they spent less time on professional development in other weeks of the term spent significantly ($p<.01$ ANOVA) more time on professional development in the recorded week than those saying that they spent about the same or more time on it in other weeks of the term.

That is to say, overall the figures from the diaries were consistent with the questionnaire answers, even though any individual could not know what the collective picture would be when he/she completed the diary and the questionnaire. It should be borne in mind that, with the considerable variation in individual teachers' workloads, there is considerable overlap between the two groups, which reduces the statistical significance achieved. This is strong evidence of internal validity in the research data.

There are also two striking examples of internal validity. We have shown in Chapter 4 that teachers who said on the questionnaire that they spent more time per week teaching their main subject actually recorded statistically significantly more time teaching their main subject ($p<.001$ linear trend) than other teachers. In Chapter 6 we showed that those with formal responsibility for pastoral care, according to the questionnaire, recorded significantly more time on it ($p<.001$ analysis of variance) than other teachers. We also showed that teachers holding responsibility for pastoral care also engaged significantly more in a range of 'welfare'-associated activities, such as liaison ($p<.05$ analysis of variance), assembly ($p<.001$ analysis of variance) and working breaks ($p<.05$ analysis of variance) than other teachers.

BIBLIOGRAPHY

Acker, S. (1987), 'Primary school teaching as an occupation', in Delamont, S. (ed.), *The Primary School Teacher*; Lewes, Falmer Press.

Acker, S. (ed.) (1989), *Teachers, Gender and Careers*; Lewes, Falmer Press.

Acker, S. (1990), 'Teachers' culture in an English primary school: continuity and change', *British Journal of Sociology of Education*, 11.3, pp. 257–73.

Acker, S. (1992), 'Teacher relationships and educational reform in England and Wales', *The Curriculum Journal*, 2.2.

Al-Khalifa, E. (1989), 'Management by halves: women teachers and school management', in DeLyon, H. and Widdowson-Migniuolo, F. (eds), *Women Teachers*; Milton Keynes, Open University Press.

Apple, M. (1986), *Teachers and Texts*; New York, Routledge & Kegan Paul.

Apple, M. and Jungck, S. (1991), 'You don't have to be a teacher to teach in this unit: teaching, technology and control in the classroom', in Hargreaves, A. and Fullan, M. (eds), *Understanding Teacher Development*; London, Cassell.

Bell, L. (1988), *Management Skills in Primary Schools*; London, Routledge.

Bennett, N. (1978), 'Recent research on teaching: a dream, a belief and a model', *British Journal of Educational Psychology*, 48.1, pp. 127–47.

Bennett, N. (1989), 'Classroom-based assessment: the National Curriculum and beyond', *Proceedings of the 2nd Annual Conference of the Association for the Study of Primary Education*; Bristol, Bristol Polytechnic.

Black, P. (1992), 'The shifting scenery of the National Curriculum', *British Association Annual Conference*, Southampton University (August).

Braverman, H. (1974), *Labour and Monopoly Capital*; New York, Monthly Review Press.

Burgess, R. (1983), *Experiencing Comprehensive Education*; London, Methuen.

Busher, H. and Saran, R. (1990), 'Teachers' morale and their conditions of service', *Annual Conference of BEMAS*; Reading, Reading University.

Byrne, E. (1978), *Women and Education*; London, Tavistock.

Callahan, R. (1962), *Education and the Cult of Efficiency*; Chicago, University of Chicago Press.

Campbell, R.J. (1992), *The Management of Teachers' Time in Primary Schools: Concepts, Evidence and Issues*, ASPE Papers; Stoke, Trentham Books.

Campbell, R.J., Evans, L., Packwood, A. and Neill, S.R.St.J. (1991), *Workloads, Achievement and Stress: Two Follow-up Studies of the Use of Teacher Time at Key Stage 1*; London, Assistant Masters' and Mistresses' Association.

Campbell, R.J. and Neill, S.R.St.J. (1990), *1330 Days: Final Report of a Pilot Study of Teacher Time at Key Stage 1*; London, Assistant Masters' and Mistresses' Association.

Campbell, R.J. and Neill, S.R.St.J. (1994), *Primary Teachers at Work*; London, Routledge.

Connell, R. (1985), *Teachers' Work*; Sidney, Allen & Unwin.

Coopers and Lybrand Deloitte (1991), *Costs of the National Curriculum in Primary Schools*; London, National Union of Teachers.

Cox, C.B. and Dyson, A.E. (1969), *The Crisis in Education: Black Paper 2*; London, Critical Quarterly.

Cox, C.B. and Dyson, A.E. (1970), *Good-bye, Mr. Short: Black Paper 3*; London, Critical Quarterly.

De Lyon, H. & Widdowson-Migniuolo, F. (eds) (1989), *Women Teachers: Issues and Experiences*; Milton Keynes, Open University Press.

Department of Education and Science (1982), *The Cockcroft Report, 'Mathematics Counts'*; London, HMSO.

Department of Education and Science (1986), Statistical Bulletin 8/86.

Department of Education and Science (1987), Statistical Bulletin 10/87.

Department of Education and Science (1989a), *School Teachers' Pay and Conditions Document*; London, HMSO.

Department of Education and Science (1989b), *Standards in Education, 1987: The Annual Report of HM Senior Chief Inspector of Schools*; London, HMSO.

Department of Education and Science (1989c), *Circular on the Length and Control of School Sessions*; London, HMSO.

Department of Education and Science (1990a), *Standards in Education, 1988–89: The Annual Report of HM Senior Chief Inspector of Schools*; London, HMSO.

Department of Education and Science (1990b), *Statistics of Education, Schools*; London, HMSO.

Department of Education and Science (1991a), *Standards in Education, 1989–90: The Annual Report of HM Senior Chief Inspector of Schools*; London, HMSO.

Department of Education and Science (1991b), *Assessment, Recording and Reporting*; London, HMSO.

Duffy, M. (1993), article in *Times Educational Supplement*, 16 July, p. 48.

Dunham, J. (1984), *Stress in Teaching*; Sydney, Croom Helm.

Earley, P. and Baker, L. (1989), *The Recruitment, Retention, Motivation and Morale of Senior Staff in Schools*; Windsor, NFER.

Earley, P. and Fletcher-Campbell, F.J. (1990), *The Time to Manage?*; Windsor, NFER/Nelson.

Etzioni, A. (ed.) (1969), *The Semi-Professions and Their Organisation*; New York, Free Press.

Evans, L., Packwood, A., Neill, S. R., St. J. Neill, S. R. and Campbell, R. J. (1994), *The Meaning of Infant Teachers' Work*; London, Routledge.

Evetts, J. (1990), *Women Teachers in Primary Education*; London, Methuen.

Fletcher-Campbell, F.J. (1988), *Middle Management in Schools – Pastoral and Academic Heads: An Annotated Bibliography*; Windsor, NFER.

Fullan, M.G. and Hargreaves, A. (1991), *What's Worth Fighting For? Working Together for Your School*; Toronto, Canada, Ontario Institute for Studies in Education.

Gallie, D. and White, M. (1993), *Employee Commitment and the Skills Revolution: Findings from The Employment in Britain Survey*; Nuffield College, Oxford.

Hargreaves, A. (1991), 'Teacher preparation time and the intensification thesis', *Annual Conference of the American Educational Research Association*; Chicago (3–7 April).

Hewitt, P. (1993), *About Time: The Revolution in Work and Family Life*; London, River Oram Press.

Hilsum, S. and Cane, B.S. (1971), *The Teacher's Day*; Windsor, NFER.

Hilsum, S. and Strong, C. (1978), *The Secondary Teacher's Day*; Windsor, NFER.

Hoyle, E. (1980), 'Professionalisation and de-professionalisation in education', in Hoyle, E. and Megarry, J. (eds), *The World Yearbook of Education: The Professional Development of Teachers*; London, Kogan Page.

Incomes Data Services (IDS) (1992), *Hours and Holidays 1992, Study 517*; London, IDS.

Interim Advisory Committee (IAC) (1990), *Third Report on Teachers' Pay and Conditions*, Cmnd 973; London, HMSO.

International Labour Office (ILO) (1981), *Report of the Joint Meeting on Conditions of Work of Teachers (1981)*; Geneva, International Labour Office.

International Labour Office (ILO) (1991), *Teachers: Challenges of the 1990s: Second Joint Meeting on Conditions of Work of Teachers (1991)*; Geneva, International Labour Office.

Knight, B. (1989), *Managing School Time*; Harlow, Longman.

Knight, B. (1991), *Designing the School Day*; Harlow, Longman.

Kyriacou, C. (1980), 'Stress, health and schoolteachers: a comparison with other professions', *Cambridge Journal of Education*, 10, pp. 154–9.

Larson, S.M. (1980), 'Proletarianisation and educated labour', *Theory and Society*, 9.1, pp. 131–75.

Lawn, M. (ed.) (1985), *The Politics of Teacher Unionism*; London, Croom Helm.

Lawn, M. and Grace, G. (eds) (1987), *Teachers: The Culture and Politics of Work*; Lewes, Falmer Press.

Lawn, M. and Ozga, J. (1988), 'The educational worker? A re-assessment of teachers', in Ozga, J. (ed.), *Schoolwork*; Milton Keynes, Open University Press.

Lee, J. (1987), 'Pride and prejudice: teachers, class and an inner city infants' school', in Lawn, M. and Grace, G. (eds), *Teachers: The Culture and Politics of Work*; Lewes, Falmer Press.

Lowe, B. (1991), *Activity Sampling*; Hull, Humberside County Council.

Maclure, M. and Marr, A. (1990), *Final Report: Teachers' Jobs and Lives*; ESRC Contract R.000231257.

McMahon, A. and Bolam, R. (1987), *School Management Development: A Handbook for LEAs*; Bristol, NDC/SMT.

Marland, M. (1971), *Head of Department*; London, Heinemann.

Marland, M. and Bayne-Jardine, C. (1986), *School Management Skills*; London, Heinemann.

Marsh, C. (1991), *Hours of Work of Women and Men in Britain*; Equal Opportunities Commission, London, HMSO.

Merson, M. (1989), 'Teacher match and education policy', *Journal of Education Policy*, 4.2, pp. 171–84.

NAS/UWT (1990), *Teacher Workload Survey*; Birmingham, NAS/UWT.

NAS/UWT (1991), *Teacher Workload Survey*; Birmingham, NAS/UWT.

National Curriculum Council/SEAC (1993), *The National Curriculum and its Assessment: An Interim Report by Sir Ron Dearing*; London, NCC/SEAC.

National Curriculum Council (1993), *National Curriculum at Key Stages 1 and 2 : Advice to the Secretary of State* (January 1993); York, NCC.

Neale, R. and Mindel, R. (1991), *Personnel Management*, quoted in *The Independent*, 31 December.

New Earnings Survey (1991), Tables 148 and 149; London, HMSO.

OECD (1990), *The Teacher Today: Tasks, Conditions, Policies*; Organisation for Economic Co-operation and Development, Paris.

OFSTED (1993), *Curriculum Organisation and Curriculum Practice in Primary Schools: A Follow-up Report*; London, HMSO.

Osborn, M. and Broadfoot, P. (1991), 'The impact of current changes in English primary schools on teacher professionalism', Annual Conference of the American Educational Research Association, Chicago.

Ozga, J. (1988) (ed.), *Schoolwork: Approaches to the Labour Process of Teaching*; Milton Keynes, Open University Press.

Ozga, J. and Lawn, M. (1981), *Teachers' Professionalism and Class*; Lewes, Falmer Press.

Ozga, J. and Lawn, M. (1988), 'Schoolwork: interpreting the labour process of teaching', *British Journal of Sociology of Education*, 9.3, pp. 323–36.

Paine, L.W. (1990), 'Chinese teachers' views of time', in Ben-Peretz, M. and Bromme, R., *The Nature of Time in Schools and Theoretical Concepts, Practitioner Perceptions*; New York, Teachers' College Press.

Poppleton, P. and Riseborough, G. (1990), 'Teaching in the mid-1980s: the centrality of work in secondary teachers' lives', *British Educational Research Journal*, 16.2, pp. 105–22.

Prais, S.J. and Wagner, K. (1985), 'School standards in England and Germany: some summary comparisons bearing on economic performance', *National Institute Economic Review*, 1.2, May, pp. 53–76.

Price, R. and Bain, G. (1988), 'The labour force', in Halsey, A. (ed.), *British Social Trends since 1900*; London, Macmillan.

Purvis, J. (1981), 'Women and teaching in the nineteenth century', in Dale, R. *et al.*, *Education and the State, Vol. 2*; Lewes, Falmer Press.

Reyes, P. (ed.) (1990), *Teachers and their Workplace*; New York, Sage.

Ryan, W. (1971), *Blaming the Victim*; New York, Vantage Books.

Salter, B. and Tapper, T. (1981), *Education, Politics and the State*; London, Grant McIntyre.

Sharpe, S. (1984), *Double Identity*; Harmondsworth, Penguin.

Sikes, P., Measor, L. and Woods, P. (1985), *Teacher Careers: Crises and Opportunities*; Lewes, Falmer Press.

Skelton, C. (1987), 'Primary teaching : women's work, men's careers', *Annual Conference of BERA*, Manchester Polytechnic.

Smithers, A. and Robinson, P. (1991), *Staffing Secondary Schools in the Nineties*; London, The Engineering Council.

Steadman, S.D., Parsons, C. and Salter, B.G. (1978), *An Inquiry into the Impact and Take-up of Schools' Council-Funded Activities: First Interim Report*; London, Schools Council.

Tomlinson, J.R.G.T. (1990), *Small, Rural and Effective*, Warwick Papers on Education Policy; Stoke, Trentham Books.

Torrington, D. and Weightman, J. (1989), *The Reality of School Management*; Oxford, Blackwell.

Troman, G. (1989), 'Testing tensions', *British Educational Research Journal*, 15.3, pp. 279–94.

Varlaam, A., Nuttall, D. and Walker, A. (1992), *What Makes Teachers Tick?: A Survey of Teacher Morale and Motivation*; London School of Economics, Centre for Educational Research.

Weightman, J. (1988), 'The managing and organizing balance: collegiality, prescription or leadership?', BEMAS Research Conference, Cardiff.

Weindling, R. and Earley, P. (1987), *Secondary Headship: The First Years*; Windsor, NFER.

White Paper (1985), *Better Schools*; London, HMSO.

White Paper (1992), *Choice and Diversity: A New Framework for Schools*, Cmnd 2021; London, HMSO.

Willis, P. (1977), *Learning to Labour*; London, Routledge & Kegan Paul.

INDEX